# Serve
## ON Purpose

# Serve
## ON Purpose

by Dr. Patrick L. Kelly

MULTICULTURAL EDUCATION MINISTRIES

ISBN: 978-1-7322962-0-6

Printed by Dockins Printing

# ENDORSEMENTS

The book, *Serve on Purpose,* written by Dr. Patrick Kelly is a tool and gift to the body of Christ. We live in a world of choices where many committed Christians have adopted a consumer mentality of shopping churches based on their felt needs. This book identifies the need for commitment. It also addresses the issues of accountability and responsibilities of committed Christianship. I believe the book, *Serve on Purpose,* is a needed catalyst for producing mature believers who are committed to a local church, the vision of the pastor, and the mission of the ministry. Bishop Patrick Kelly has done an excellent job disseminating the information we need for strengthening the local church.

—Bryan Cutshall, Th.D.
President of Church Trainer
Chancellor of International School of the Word
Cleveland, TN

This volume is a useful tool that sheds light on the role of members in the local church. It is a must read for every pastor and a welcomed guide for members.

—Roy Notice, D.Min.
Lead Pastor Waltham Park NTCOG
Kingston, Jamaica

These gentle reminders of committed Christians' responsibilities and community influence should be taught and/or revisited in the local church on a regular basis.

—Bishop K.P. Hardemon
FL-Cocoa, Church of God
Christian Education Director

Serve on Purpose is a stellar document with wide-ranging implications for church growth. Its pages sound a resonant chord in the symphonic discourse of Christian formation.

—Dr. Wayne Solomon
Adjunct Professor
Lee University, Cleveland, TN

Serve on Purpose—a book written by Bishop Patrick L. Kelly is a gold mine of spiritual knowledge that just got tapped. Every church member needs a copy.

—Daniel J. Vassell Sr., D.Min.
Multicultural Education Ministries Coordinator
Church of God, Cleveland, TN

Many churchgoers believe that the life and ministry of a local church is a responsibility of God and the leading of a pastoral team. Yet, Patrick L. Kelly argues that a healthy church also requires the commitment of those who call that community home.

We are not called by God to a particular community of faith to be served; we are also called to be colaborers.

—Wilmer Estrada-Carrasquillo, Ph.D.
Acting Director
Center for Latino Studies
Pentecostal Theological Seminary
Church of God, Cleveland TN

I have read and thoroughly checked the content in this book, and I am very happy to read such a great work. I highly recommend this material to all the local churches and believe that it will bring a great productive and fruitful service in the local church and community.

—Dr. Samkutty Varghese
Lead Pastor
Tyner Church of God
Chattanooga, TN

# DEDICATION

This book is first and foremost dedicated to the congregations that allowed me to shepherd them, and it provided the context for the development of the principles and teachings that are presented herein: East Toronto Church of God in Canada, Cathedral of Faith in Bridgeport, Connecticut, and Cathedral Church of God in Deerfield Beach, Florida.

It is dedicated to my wife, Nicola, and my daughters, Chayanne and Sela who have been loyal and effective members of each local church that I served as pastor. And, finally, it is dedicated to the denomination that gave me the platform to serve as a pastor—the Church of God. It is a movement that empowers members to serve as ministers in the Kingdom.

# PREAMBLE

As members of the body of Christ, Christians' lives are worth much more than we can imagine or think; although, sometimes we might not feel or think so. The good news is, our worth is not measured by our feelings or thinking. On the other hand, our imaginations are limited, and our brains are not capable of comprehending the things God has in store for us (Jeremiah 1:5 and 29:11). The limitation in knowing all that God has for us—the innate drive that tells us we were created for a specific purpose in this generation—has not been removed.

Knowing the purpose God has for us is an ongoing desire of a child of God. His purpose for our lives is revealed through His Word and the relationship we have with Him.

Having the right relationship with God will cause us to live our lives with purpose in mind, and it will motivate us to live beyond our own limitations—through love, sacrifice, and in service to others.

God's purpose for our lives is not hidden from the child of God. It is written in the Book—the Bible! In the first book of the Bible, it is recorded that human beings were created in the image of God.

> And God said, "Let us make man in our image, after our likeness: and let them have dominion over the fish of the sea, and over the fowl of the air, and over the cattle, and over all the earth, and

over every creeping thing that creepeth upon the earth" (Genesis 1:26-27).

Because we are created in the image of God, we as children become God bearers. We reflect godly characteristics of love, joy, and peace. We show forth the image of God, as we display godly traits. What we read helps us to develop the character of God, so we can FINSH the great commands of God.

To help us, particularly our laity, fulfill God's purpose for our lives, Ministerial Development and School of Ministry are releasing one book per year as a resource to provide ongoing education and discipleship for our lay members.

For more than one hundred years, the Church of God has been providing educational training to laity and ministers, so that we can all rightly divide the Word of God and apply it to our lives, situations, and ministries. The books will provide spiritual development, enhancement, and resourcing for our laity. The book will be available in different languages, in paperback, and ebooks.

The purpose or goal for these books will be to provide ongoing resources for our laity in the USA and around the world to help us FINSH the Great Commission.

The Church of God is now in more than 185 countries, and we would like to offer all our members the same training and resources as best we can.

We have chosen this book, *Serve on Purpose,* as our first book to affirm and/or reaffirm one of the purposes of God's children in this world.

Many Christians think the ultimate purpose in life is the pursuit of happiness. Our ultimate purpose is: God wants His children to serve Him now in this world and live with Him forever in the world to come! This purpose involves our lives now, and it is also an awesome, unbelievable future.

*Many thinkers and scientists have been trying for years to explain purpose. Among them are the following two notable scholars:*

- Carl Gustav Jung, a Swiss psychiatrist and psychoanalyst, who founded analytical psychology, describes purpose as follows:

  > As far as we can discern, the sole purpose of human existence is to kindle a light of meaning in the darkness of mere being.

- John T. Chirban, Ph.D., Th.D., writing in *Psychology Today,* "Discovering Your Purpose: The Voyage of Self-Awareness," says,

  > Purpose is the genuine peace and contentment that comes from the authentic relationships we forge. Not simply a by-product of everyday interactions, our purpose is the result of long-term relationships that are both strengthening and affirming. Finding our purpose thus requires attunement to the needs of the crucial relationships in our life.

Both psychologists concur that our purpose includes a light and relationships which influence others. The light mentioned by Jung represents the image of God and the transforming relationships are anchored in being the image of God.

As we fulfill God's purpose for our lives as image bearers, we will wake up each morning feeling purpose-driven. Our first purpose and meaning in this life is about our relationship with God the Father and Jesus Christ. It's about being God's child now while looking forward to the promised future.

As God's children, we want to know that at the end of our lives we can say like the apostle Paul:

> For I am now ready to be offered, and the time of my departure is at hand.   I have fought a good fight, I have finished my course, I have kept the faith: Henceforth there is laid up for me a crown of righteousness, which the Lord, the righteous judge, shall give me at that day: and not to me only, but unto all them also that love his appearing (2 Timothy 4:6-8).

And others can say of me like was said of King David in the Book of Acts, he served the purpose of God in his own generation (see Acts 13:36).

David was one of the most unlikely candidates to replace King Saul. If it had been up to the prophet Samuel or Jesse, David's father, he would not have been chosen. However, he was chosen by God. He was groomed for his leadership while still a shepherd taking care of his father's sheep. God chose and ordained him and released him at the right time to replace Saul. Sure, David was not perfect. In his fallenness and weaknesses, God made David into a great king for His glory.

It is also said of David that he was a man after God's own heart. I trust that it will be said of you, at the end of your lives, that you were men and women after God's own heart, and that you fulfilled the purpose of God in your generation.

14

The challenge before you is to face the opportunities and obstacles that God has for you in your time. We don't know if these are the best of times or the worst of times. All we know is that they are your times. And God is raising up a generation of people for Himself.

The ultimate goal of these books is to enrich us to be what God purposes for us to be—God bearers . . . individually and corporately. He wants us to be God bearers at home, at church, in the community, at school, or in the workplace. Our first book will look at how we become God bearers in the church. As you prepare to read about your purpose to serve, please note what Kurt Skelly posted on January 28, 2014:

## TEN REASONS TO BE MORE INVOLVED IN LOCAL CHURCH MINISTRY

1. Glorifying God by serving in my local church ministry is the purpose of my salvation.

2. I have been uniquely gifted to serve.

3. Ministry service will demonstrate the reality of my faith.

4. The laborers are few.

5. Children tend to emulate what they see, not what they hear.

6. The Commission is great.

7. Ministry involvement enhances biblical understanding.

8. Doing anonymous or little-noticed things for the Lord is like whispering, "I love you."

9. I will forge long-lasting and valuable friendships.

10. I will stand before the Lord.

# CONTENTS

Acknowledgments ........................................................ 19

Foreword .................................................................... 21

Introduction ............................................................... 23

**Chapters**
1.  Committed Christians Support the Church ... 27
2.  Committed Christians Commit to Promote
    the Church............................................................ 39
3.  Committed Christians Defend the Church..... 55
4.  Committed Christians Maintain the Unity
    of the Fellowship ................................................ 71
5.  Committed Christians Honor and Support
    Church Leadership ............................................. 85
6.  Committed Christians Work in Harmony
    With the Local Church ....................................... 99
7.  Committed Christians Serve for the Glory
    of God ................................................................ 111
8.  Conclusion ......................................................... 121

# ACKNOWLEDGMENTS

I am grateful for those who have impacted me and rightfully share in the production of this material.

To my wife, Nicola, who has been a constant source of encouragement and my daughters, Chayanne and Sela, who are burgeoning writers themselves, and inspire me to chart a path for them to follow. Thanks to my parents, Levi and Leslin, who exposed me to the things of God and the culture of the church at an early age; and C. Molin, who edited and critiqued the draft manuscript, and challenged me to think through some of the concepts that are presented in this book.

Special thanks to the Church of God Division of Education copy editor, Nellie Keasling for her editorial expertise; to Lonna Gattenby for flowing the book and the graphic art.

# FOREWORD

C hristians celebrate Pentecost, the gift of the Holy Spirit, 50 days after the resurrection of Christ. Pentecost is regarded as the birthday of the Christian church, and the start of the church's mission to the world. When a large crowd gathered in Jerusalem, curious about what they heard and saw after a small group of prayerful Christ-followers was baptized in the Holy Spirit, the apostle Peter stepped forward and began to preach.

> "Those who believed what Peter said were baptized and added to the church that day—about 3,000 in all" (Acts 2:41 NLT).

When the message of Christ's death, burial, and resurrection was proclaimed, the New Testament church was born! The 21st-century church looks very different around the world. There are churches with steeples and pews; churches in homes and open-air pavilions; and services held in commercial buildings and public facilities. So, what is the church? *We are* the church of the living God—those who come together weekly in community worship and service. *You and I* are the church.

Local committed Christians hip carries privileges and responsibilities. We unite in heart and purpose to proclaim the good news, offer a place of safety and refuge for those hurting and in need of salvation, and to provide training and instruction for all generations to grow in the knowledge and understanding of Scripture.

Spiritual health in committed Christians produces a strong and vibrant church that supports the needs of congregation—from the cradle to the grave—and reaches beyond the walls of a structure and draws the "unchurched" into fellowship, a new hope, and a future in Christ Jesus.

A manual is defined as a small book, giving information, instructions, or guidance. May the scriptures outlined in this booklet, encourage you in your walk with Christ and to greater service and fulfillment through committed Christians hip.

The one thing I ask of the Lord— the thing I seek most—
is to live in the house of the Lord all the days of my life,
delighting in the Lord's perfections
and meditating in his Temple.
For he will conceal me there when troubles come;
he will hide me in his sanctuary.
He will place me out of reach on a high rock.
Then I will hold my head high
above my enemies who surround me.
At his sanctuary I will offer sacrifices with shouts of joy,
singing and praising the Lord with music
(Psalm 27:4-6 NLT).

*—David E. Ramírez, D.Min.*
*Church of God*
*Assistant General Overseer*
*Divisional Director of Education*

# INTRODUCTION

A sk any church member what the job of a pastor entails, and you will no doubt receive a litany of responses that include preaching, praying for the sick, counseling individuals and couples, and officiating at weddings and funerals. Anyone who has spent a considerable amount of time in the culture of the church will have been exposed to the functions of the pastor and likely have an opinion as to what the job involves.

Since it is a Scriptural activity, there is much information in the Bible that outlines what God's shepherds are expected to do in service to the body of Christ. In addition, numerous books, articles and papers have been written that elaborate upon the duties and expectations of the pastor. And finally, the well-trained minister is one who has Bible school, college or seminary training aimed at thoroughly preparing for the pastoral role.

If one were to determine the duties of a local church member, however, one would probably be at a loss as to specific and definite information regarding that role and function within the church. The Bible provides much information about who the Christian is and what the Christian should do, but there is nothing that addresses the idea of local committed Christians hip.

The view of the New Testament writers was that there was one growing church with believers in the various cities where the gospel message was accepted. As such, the instructions given to one geographical group were often directed toward Christians in other areas as well. In the history of church development, it was only with the rise of different denominations that local committed Christians hip took on any meaning at all. As people identified themselves with a specific church, then membership brought distinction. It gave individuals a sense of community and provided organizations with a base for support.

But even then, there is not much information on actual membership, outside of doctrinal practices and beliefs relative to an independent church, affiliated groups of churches, or a denomination. Membership classes in most churches consist of merely familiarizing newcomers with the vision, values, and policies of the local church. Specific information that may be considered transferable from one church to another is almost nonexistent regarding the actual duties of a member. Is it any wonder then that many churchgoers approach attendance with a consumer mentality?

The privileges and benefits of membership are the emphasis when one is examining the various opportunities among local churches. These are the days where many select where they will worship based upon the question, "What does this church offer?" The idea of participation and cooperation with a local assembly is secondary to the issue of getting a return for one's time and money.

Among the many benefits of membership in a local assembly of believers is the fact that it provides a community or family in which to share and experience fellowship with other Christians. It provides personal access to godly instruction for one's spiritual growth, stimulates faith to believe for God's best in one's life, and is a resource for strength and support in times of pain and trial. In addition, the local church grants a spiritual covering, especially in the exercising of one's gifts in ministry. The New Testament clearly demonstrates the link between one's spiritual development and involvement in the church. There is no doubt, then, that membership comes with certain built-in benefits and privileges, but alongside of them must be the understanding of responsibilities and duties as well.

The purpose of this book is to provide much needed information relative to the function of a church member. The idea of partnership and cooperation with the local church resonates throughout the seven responsibilities detailed here. With the proper perspective of committed Christians hip as an opportunity to covenant with and serve the body of Christ through a local ministry, greater productivity in the Kingdom can be accomplished.

The consumer-minded approach to church attendance can be minimized while a deeper level of commitment and service can be reached. Every congregation can benefit from a greater awareness among its membership when *discipleship* is defined as "a call to service." God, His church, and our fellow man are to be the objects of our service, and the local church has been designed by God to accomplish that purpose. *Serve on Purpose* will enable individuals to know exactly what is expected of them and to thereby be equipped for maximum productivity in the local church.

There is an urgent sense of fulfilling the Great Commission, properly identified as the FINISH Commitment, guiding the focus and actions of many church organizations across denominational lines today. There is a renewed sense of purpose, among local congregations, to reap the harvest in anticipation of our Lord's soon return. The work of reaping and finishing will be aided by churches properly positioned to obey the Lord's command. The positioning of the local church is affected by the awareness of its membership of the responsibilities that will make its work successful.

# Chapter 1

# COMMITTED CHRISTIANS
# SUPPORT THE CHURCH

"You know about Stephanas and his family; they are
the first Christian converts in Achaia and have *given
themselves to the service* of God's people"
(1 Cor. 16:15 GNT).

Maturing members of the local church will recognize they are not there just to derive blessings and benefits from the church, but to be a blessing and a benefit to the church as well. The New Testament offers some practical advice to believers which can be appropriately applied to membership in the church regarding the support of the ministry. For example, Paul urges the Corinthian church to pursue unity (1 Cor. 1:10) at a time when divisions among the brethren were jeopardizing the proclamation of the gospel and the stability of the church. His urgent response to their behavior was intended to correct wrong attitudes and put them back on the path to a Christ-centered perspective.

Every member of the local church is important to the body of Christ in general and the local church in particular. The impact of the Christian worldview upon society is dependent, in part, upon each believer's actions in society. And the effectiveness of any local church will be directly related to the level of support given by its membership. Believers should be faithful to the cause of Christ in the world and, as committed Christians, should be faithful to the local church in its pursuit of the causes of Christ. There are three main areas of support—time, talent, and treasure—that all individuals are called upon and expected to provide for the success of the local church.

## TIME

Membership in the local church requires an investment of that valuable commodity known as time. Attendance at worship services, Bible studies, small group meetings, choir and praise team rehearsals, ministry training sessions, and a host of other activities demand the willingness of committed Christians to be there to participate. In fact, the very nature of the body of Christ is such that interconnectedness and interaction among the various members for the accomplishment of the directives of the body are a foregone conclusion. The presence and partnership of all members are therefore undeniably necessary. The writer of Hebrews speaks profoundly to the issue of church attendance and participation.

> Let us be concerned for one another, to help one another to show love and to do good. Let us not give up the habit of meeting together, as some are doing. Instead, let us encourage one another all the more. (Heb. 10:24-25 GNT).

28

To encourage and help each other, believers were expected and urged to attend the various meetings of the church. Apparently, this statement was stimulated by noticeable absences in church gatherings. Persecution of Christians during the time was perhaps causing some to stay away in fear. Corporate gatherings were the more necessary for mutual encouragement. The early church believers in Jerusalem demonstrated an understanding of the investment of time for both benefit and blessing. Their actions portray a people who were unselfish in their pursuit of the newfound relationship they had discovered in Jesus Christ. Unity, harmony, and agreement characterized their attitude and behavior in the initial stages of the church's development and growth.

> And they continued steadfastly in the apostle's doctrine and fellowship, and in breaking of bread, and in prayers. . . . And they, continuing daily with one accord in the temple and breaking bread from house to house, did eat their meat with gladness and singleness of heart (Acts 2:42, 46 KJV).

Every church should strive to possess those characteristics in its membership, and every member should demonstrate that kind of commitment. With all the demands being made upon our time in an increasingly busy society, we should never forget to give time to the things that are truly important and lasting. One's spiritual life and expression should be given priority in the ordering of our lives. Spiritual growth and discipleship include participation in the local church. The giving of one's time enables mutual interaction and development, and enhances the efforts of the church. But the investment of time is not just to support the church with one's attendance, but also with one's influence. Influence should be understood here as the positive impact that one's presence and participation will have upon others. As members interact with each other in the local church context, growth and development are stimulated by the influence of each upon the other. Mutual encouragement through testimony, exhortation, worship, and even prayer mark the path to spiritual maturity.

> Let the word of Christ richly dwell within you, with all wisdom teaching and admonishing one another with psalms and hymns and spiritual songs, singing with thankfulness in your hearts to God (Col. 3:16 NASB).

> This is what I mean, my friends. When you meet for worship, one person has a hymn, another a teaching, another a revelation from God, another a message in strange tongues, and still another the explanation of what is said. Everything must be of help to the church (1 Cor. 14:26 GNT).

> Finally, all of you be of one mind, having compassion for one another; love as brothers, be tender-hearted, be courteous; not returning evil for evil or reviling for reviling, but on the contrary blessing, knowing that you were called to this, that you may inherit a blessing (1 Pet. 3:8-9).

With these considerations, then, committed Christians are encouraged to show support for the local church by giving their time to the various functions of the ministry. Attendance and visibility at the church and in the various programs are one of the ways members can demonstrate a vibrant relationship with God, as well as reveal an understanding of Christian responsibility. Timely, consistent, and committed participation will be of great benefit to both the individual and to the church.

## TALENT

The second area of support committed Christians ought to provide for the success of the local church efforts involves the exercising of personal and spiritual gifts, and talents. All of us have been endowed by God with abilities that distinguish us from others because of the ease with which we are able to demonstrate them. Some have the remarkable ability to sing, using their voices as an instrument in itself; others have keen minds for organizing and planning; while still others may be gifted in the use of their hands to create, maintain, or repair. Without a doubt, every human being has the potential to be good at something and many possess multiple talents. The discovery and use of these talents and natural abilities tend to give a sense of purpose and satisfaction, especially when they are performed for the benefit of others.

The local church ministry is the expression of individual talents and abilities collectively engaged for Kingdom purposes; therefore, the talents of the committed Christians are necessary for effective ministry. In the Old Testament, Moses was instructed to build a Tabernacle using the skilled craftsmen in the congregation of Israel. His statements reveal an understanding that these individuals were positioned where they were to be of service to the work of God.

> All who are gifted artisans among you shall come
> and make all that the Lord has commanded. . . .
> And Moses said to the children of Israel "See, the

> Lord has called by name Bezalel the son of Uri,
> the son of Hur, of the tribe of Judah; and He has
> filled him with the Spirit of God, in wisdom and
> understanding, in knowledge and all manner of
> workmanship, to design artistic works, to work
> in gold and silver and bronze, in cutting jewels
> for setting, in carving wood, and to work in all
> manner of artistic workmanship" (Exod. 35:10,
> 30-33).

The New Testament Scriptures affirm that one's abilities are given by God for the specific purpose of serving in His church. And committed Christians are to demonstrate responsible stewardship of God's gifts by exercising them for God's glory.

> As each one has received a special gift, employ
> it in serving one another as good stewards of the
> manifold grace of God (1 Pet. 4:10 NASB).
>
> Even so ye, forasmuch as ye are zealous of spir-
> itual gifts, seek that ye may excel to the edifying
> of the church (1 Cor. 14:12 KJV).

The parable of the talents in Matthew 25:14-30 teaches that believers are expected to use what they have been given and that they will be rewarded accordingly.

> His Lord said to him, "Well done, good and faith-
> ful servant; you have been faithful over a few
> things, I will make you ruler over many things.
> Enter into the joy of your Lord" (Matt. 25:23).

Several things are to be noted from a reading of this parable. First, each servant was given talents that were the property of the master (Matt. 25:14). Whatever abilities we possess do not originate with us, but they have been given to us by God. If this were not the case, we could simply choose our own gifts at will and exercise them. The reality is that if you were not born with some natural proclivity toward singing, then all of the training in the world would never make you an opera virtuoso. You can work only with what you have, and what you have is what you have been given. Hence, we are merely stewards of the gifts or talents that we possess.

Second, each servant was given talents in accordance with his ability (Matt. 25:15). From this we can determine that our responsibilities are to be connected to our abilities (talents and gifts) to manage them. Hence, people skilled in the use of their hands would probably not fare as well if they were given a task that required administrative oversight. Give them an assignment suited to their natural abilities, however, and they will astound you with their precision and craftsmanship. If they have been blessed to excel in both the work of their hands and their minds, being multitalented, then their usefulness and productivity increased tremendously.

Third, the servants were expected to use what they had been given in service to the master (Matt. 25:19). Our talents and gifts are ultimately for the purpose of glorifying God by using them as He determines and not for our own desires. It is possible to possess a gift or talent and use it selfishly and incorrectly. The text here is instructive regarding the issue: For, the one servant buried his talent (put it away as he saw fit to do) and was rebuked for it. At the issuance of the talent, it was understood that he was to make good use of it for the master. Certainly, his fellow servants carried out their duties and accomplished what was expected. But this one was accused of being wicked and lazy, ultimately dishonoring his master and losing his talent and reward.

Our churches can provide a stronger witness and accomplish the various tasks of evangelism, discipleship, fellowship, worship, and ministry when members use their gifts in service to the Lord. In times past, the model of local church ministry used to be that of the minister, secretary, and a few deacons doing the work, but new paradigms are emerging that promote the necessity of maximum participation for maximum productivity. The Pareto Principle established that 80 percent of the people do 20 percent of the work while 20 percent of the people do 80 percent of the work. Those figures can be changed to reflect greater productivity from the greater participation of the membership, if "saved to serve" becomes the rallying cry of our congregations.

## TREASURE

The third area of member support for the local church has to do with finances or treasure. This involves the giving of tithes, offerings, and special monetary gifts to the local ministry effort. It goes without saying that ministry costs money. Buildings, maintenance, missions, outreach, education, training, fellowship, benevolence, etc. cannot take place if there is no financial support derived from the members of the church. Thankfully, Scripture speaks to the issue in clear terms and provides a framework within which members can be encouraged to give of their treasure. Just as with the talents that we possess, biblical stewardship affirms that God owns everything, He graciously gives us what we have, He expects us to give back to Him, and He attaches a promise of further blessing for our obedience in giving in accordance with His will.

That God is the owner of all earth's resources is clearly established in the Old Testament:

> The earth is the Lord's, and the fullness thereof; the world, and they that dwell therein (Psalm 24:1; see also Psalm 50:10 and Hag. 2:8).

Since God is the owner of everything, He is the source of all that we attain or possess.

> But thou shalt remember the Lord thy God: for it is he that giveth thee power to get wealth (Deut. 8:18 KJV; see also Psalm 145:15-16 and John 3:27).

Although God gives to us, He asks that we give back a portion of what we receive.

> Speak to the children of Israel, that they bring me an offering. From everyone who gives it willingly with his heart you shall take my offering (Exod. 25:2; see also Lev. 27:30 and Deut. 16:17).

Our obedience to give as God directs releases the promise of His provision in our lives.

> Honor the Lord with your possessions, and with the firstfruits of all your increase; so your barns will be filled with plenty, and your vats will overflow with new wine. (Prov. 3: 9-10; see also Prov. 11:25 and Luke 6:38).

There are various instances in Scripture where the people of God were instructed to give for the support of godly initiatives, the functions of the temple, or specific tasks.

*For the building of the temple*: "They gave for the work of the house of God five thousand talents and ten thousand darics of gold, ten thousand talents of silver, eighteen thousand talents of bronze, and one hundred thousand talents of iron" (1 Chron. 29:7).

*For the functions of the temple*: "Bring all the tithes into the storehouse, that there may be food in My house" (Mal. 3:10).

*Benevolence for the poor*: "On the first day of the week let each one of you lay something aside, storing up as he may prosper, that there be no collections when I come" (1 Cor. 16:2).

Each church will have specific opportunities and means for the members to contribute in accordance with the biblical standards. These will include tithing, offerings, pledges, and special donations. In addition, fundraising initiatives and activities are to be found in abundance in many churches whether it be car washes, barbeque dinners, musicals, cookbooks, bake sales, or shopping excursions.

It must be understood, however, that it is the financial partnership of the individual member with the local church that enables the ministry to survive and function. Regular, faithful giving to the local church will result in fiscal stability for the ministry, the continued provision of God in the life of the member, and resources to pursue the fulfillment of the Great Commission mandate to proclaim the gospel to the world.

## MEMBERSHIP ASSESSMENT
- Are you giving consistent, quality time to the ministries of your local church?
- Are you using your gifts in service to your local church?
- Do you regularly give tithes and offerings in your local church?

## A FINAL CONSIDERATION
Bridgeport Connecticut is home to Cathedral of Faith Church of God, a thriving and influential ministry in the city and community. Founded in 1980 by a small group of believers meeting in a living room, the ministry's beginning was humble but promising. Growth soon necessitated larger accommodations, which were secured in 1981 with the rental of a facility on Colorado Avenue.

According to the congregation's official historical record,

> The resulting increase in membership soon presented the need for even more room for the thriving congregation. The decision was made to purchase a building that would provide for future growth as well as immediate growth and, in 1985, under the leadership of pastor Martin Wright, a derelict building at 2319 Fairfield Avenue became the new home of the (then) Bridgeport Church of God. The excited believers threw themselves into the dauting task of cleaning and refurbishing the building. Everyone, including the children, joined in to improve the property and make it suitable for worship. The result was expedited ministry that produced steady growth in membership from the low 100s in 1985 to more than 300 in 1992.

Ten years later, the church again found itself in need of larger accommodations. "In early 2002, Bishop Kelly (pastor at the time) fostered a daring plan of fundraising" to enable the construction of a new building. "Each member/partner was asked to bring an offering equal to one week's salary on the fifth Sunday of each month. According to his projections, each quarter would yield $35,000 for the building fund with a year-end total of $140,000.

> The first Super Sunday, as Bishop Kelly dubbed it, saw the people give over $37,000 on Easter Sunday. This was almost double the amount brought in (for the building fund) during all the previous year. Needless to say, the excitement level was raised to a feverish high. This approach was repeated in 2003, and the overall results were similar. In both years the totals exceeded the minimum of $100,000 by the end of December.

In both instances, the refurbishing of the original building in 1985, and giving toward the construction of a new edifice in 2002, the congregation demonstrated support for the church. They gave of their time, talents, and treasure to accomplish the objectives of the ministry. The same approach described the service of the members in the various ministries that the church engaged in as well. Musicians, choirs, ushers, teachers, technicians and other volunteer positions were filled by willing, able, and committed members of the church. Bridgeport Church of God grew back then, and Cathedral of Faith continues to thrive and benefit today, due to the support of its loyal members.

# Chapter 2

# COMMITTED CHRISTIANS COMMIT TO PROMOTE THE CHURCH

"That you may become blameless and harmless,
children of God without fault in the midst
of a crooked and perverse generation,
*among whom you shine as lights in the world"*
(Phil. 2:15).

The promotion and advancement of the church in the world is part of God's redemptive plan. Both testaments of Scripture reveal that God calls out a people unto Himself for relationship and fellowship and to reveal Himself to the wider world through that group of people. The church is comprised of those who have acknowledged, turned to, and embraced God and His love. The sharing of God's unconditional love and mercy through His Son Jesus Christ to those who have not heard is what enables the growth and progress of God's kingdom. Every local expression of the church will inevitably seek to fulfill its role in proclaiming and promoting the gospel, thereby advancing the church and the kingdom of God.

The active participation of the local church in God's plan of redemption is revealed in the Great Commission mandate of Matt. 28:18-20 and Mark 16:15-18. It is realized in the behavior of the apostles who, after Christ's ascension, "went out and preached everywhere, the Lord working with them and confirming the word through the accompanying signs" (Mark 16:20). And it is confirmed in the actions of the early church in Acts after Pentecost and after persecution. In each instance, they took the gospel message to the various communities and cities where they found themselves. And in each instance, their influence was seen in the many conversions to Christ and the establishment of local churches.

This partnership of the local assembly with God in the promotion of His church is greatly facilitated through the involvement of an informed and willing membership. Alongside ministries that cater to the development of the believer's faith, there must be initiatives that encourage members to share their faith, represent God in society, and proclaim the gospel to an unbelieving world. It must be understood by the local membership that it is their duty to engage in activities that communicate God's love to the surrounding community and world.

As the early church believers lived out their faith by honoring Christ and testifying to His lordship, they were, in effect, promoting the church. As His representatives, believers today are engaged in the same activity. One need not hold a title, position, or ministerial credential to participate in promoting the church. A simple cognizance of one's potential to affect a person's eternal destiny, along with a willingness to be used by the Holy Spirit is sufficient to carry out the duty. And though promotion of the church can take many forms, they can generally be grouped into two categories—godly influence and lifestyle evangelism.

## PROMOTING THE CHURCH THROUGH GODLY INFLUENCE (IN THE WORLD)

There can be no doubt that the influence of godly people has had a dramatic effect on nations and people of the world throughout history. Scripture records that whole cities turned to the Lord at the preaching of the apostles in the Book of Acts. The same acceptance of the gospel message brought peace and prosperity to those nations that had respect for the church in the early centuries. It can be argued that Spain, Britain, and America attained the heights of world dominance only after they submitted to God. And the establishment of numerous social welfare institutions came about through those who sought to express God's love to a hurting humanity. All of this can be attributed to the influential attitudes, perspectives, and behavior of men and women who revered God in both private and public spheres.

In His Sermon on the Mount, Jesus teaches many things concerning the kingdom of God and its citizens. He gives specific information regarding the behavior that is expected of those who serve God. In many instances that godly behavior goes against popular trend and even personal preference. Rather it pushes one to a level of selflessness and altruism rarely displayed in normal societal interaction. Jesus' statements in Matthew 5 reveal just how valuable and significant His followers are in the world.

> You are the salt of the earth; but if the salt loses its flavor, how shall it be seasoned? It is then good for nothing but to be thrown out and trampled underfoot by men (Matt. 5:13).

If salt is an important condiment and ingredient for us today, it was even more important for ancient society. In biblical times, salt was derived from the earth and was intermingled with minerals and vegetable matter. In the absence of refrigeration and modern methods of food preservation, it was invaluable in preventing meat from spoiling. Likewise, the church exists in the world as a preserving influence against the ravages of sin and godlessness. The message and practice of the church always point man to high ethical standards, morality, brotherhood, and compassion. Without this message and action countering selfishness, immorality, and un-righteousness, the world would be utterly given over to evil.

Committed Christians act as salt in the world by living a disciplined and godly lives among unbelievers. By wholly following God in submission and obedience, believers point unbelievers to a higher level of living. By practicing the principles of their Christian faith, they offer an attractive and effective counter to the manifestations of sin and unrighteousness in the world. Paul's encouragement to the believers at Thessalonica, who were being led to believe that the Day of the Lord had already come, points to the preserving nature of the Holy Spirit's work in the world through the church.

> For the mystery of lawlessness is already at work; only He who now restrains will do so until he is taken out of the way. And then the lawless one

> will be revealed, whom the Lord will consume
> with the breath of His mouth and destroy with
> the brightness of His coming (2 Thess. 2:7-8).

Salt was also used as a purifier in ancient times and maintains that quality today. Wounds could be kept from infection by the application of salt. Skin could be exfoliated and cleansed by rubbing with salt. And a mouthwash of salt water could help sores to heal quickly. Committed Christians demonstrate a purifying influence in the world by proclaiming the gospel and leading men to the cleansing power of Christ's blood. The stain of sin is revealed in man's continued rebellion against God and the pursuit of unrighteousness. The only remedy is the applied blood of Jesus Christ as seen in the transformed life of the Christian (i.e. church member).

> Therefore, if anyone is in Christ, he is a new cre-
> ation; old things have passed away; behold, all
> things have become new (2 Cor. 5:17).

Another noteworthy fact about salt is that it penetrates and makes its presence known. The addition of salt to a meal, for example, is generally unmistakable. It has an overwhelming influence on what it comes into contact with. Likewise, the church penetrates society as believers/members bring their transformed lifestyles into the workplace, school, business, and community of which they are part. Though they may appear to blend in with their surroundings, the power of God at work within them will inevitably draw attention and provoke a reaction. Believers have been found in every facet and at every level of society, be it education, politics, business, industry, military, music, or entertainment. As a result, the influence of the church can be felt almost everywhere. Jesus' follow-up to the salt of the earth comparison speaks even more profoundly to the church's influence.

> You are the light of the world. A city that is set on a hill cannot be hidden. Nor do they light a lamp and put it under a basket, but on a lampstand, and it gives light to all who are in the house. Let your light so shine before men, that they may see your good works and glorify your Father in heaven (Matt. 5:14-16).

This revelation confirms the necessity of the church in the world as the agency of God's redemptive work. The believers who comprise the church are the light of the world. They are the possessors of that light source that dispels the darkness and reveals the truth. As a light bulb turned on in a dark room illuminates and enables one to navigate, so too does the church have the task of showing the way to those who are in darkness. These verses speak to the prominence, the power, and the purpose of the church.

As the light of the world and a city set on a hill, the church is visible and unavoidably prominent. It cannot be ignored or dismissed because it has been positioned where it is in the world by God himself. Its influence will be inevitable because of its placement. It makes no sense for the local church to confine itself to the four walls of its sanctuary when God has positioned the body of Christ in a place of prominence. Its influence must be felt and seen in the local community by the active participation of its membership in society.

Second, the power of the church is revealed in the function of light. When the light is turned on, those who are in the house can see and benefit from its illumination. As small and insignificant as a candle may seem during daylight, its value and power are greatly appreciated in the midst of darkness. As the light of the world, it is the church that has the power to illuminate and reveal truth. The importance of education, science, and philosophy cannot be denied, but it is the church that has been endowed with the influence of absolute truth. That same truth has, throughout history, informed educational, scientific, and philosophical pursuits. That's the awesome and undeniable power of the church.

Third, the purpose of the church, as the light of the world, is to illuminate in such a way that men glorify God. Through good works and righteous living among men, the believer points the unbeliever toward God. As representatives of the Kingdom, we are to testify of and give witness to Jesus Christ. We are to honor and exalt Him in all of our ways. In so doing, we are placed on display for the world to see with the intent that the unbeliever becomes influenced to come and join us in the Kingdom and thus give glory to God. A beacon on the ocean's shore points the way to port for the uncertain sailor and results in thanksgiving when the ship arrives safely. The end result of illumination by the church is that men would know and celebrate God.

When believers (committed Christians) yield to God's design, they can then assume the responsibility of being a proper influence in the local community. Their attitudes and actions will promote the body of Christ at large and the local church in particular. They will be like salt permeating, preserving, and purifying the community and world in which they live. They will be like that illuminated city on a hill. Men will be drawn to the unavoidable light that they possess and glorify God.

## PROMOTING THE CHURCH THROUGH LIFESTYLE EVANGELISM

If the end result of the committed Christian's godly influence in the community is that unbelievers come to know God, then it is even more so the direct objective of lifestyle evangelism. This is where believers intentionally develop relationships with unbelievers, to introduce them to Christ. The relationship provides the context of friendship, confidence, and trust that make the presentation and acceptance of the gospel less intimidating. In fact, believers live out the gospel so that their actions, more than their words, communicate the message of God's redemptive love. By providing an up close and personal interaction with the Christian experience, the potential barriers and objections of the unbeliever are rendered ineffective. Out of all the evangelistic methods used in Christian ministry, lifestyle evangelism has proven most effective at promoting Christ, as well as His church, both universal and local. It can even be argued that the growth and proliferation of the church throughout history was facilitated through transformed individuals interacting with those closest to them and leading them to faith in Christ.

One of the obvious and most convenient relationships wherein believers can engage lifestyle evangelism is in their families. Unsaved relatives come with an established familiarity and trust that usually make sharing the gospel easy. Changes in believers' lives that have occurred because of the power of Christ are more readily seen and appreciated by family members who know them intimately. Committed Christians should purposefully live out their faith in front of their families and seize the opportunity to demonstrate the Christian life. They should regularly pray for and encourage their unsaved family members to surrender their lives to Jesus Christ. They should invite and bring them to their local church for worship, fellowship, and instruction in the things of God.

The Scriptures indicate that many individuals effectively introduced their family members to the gospel by way of their relationship. In the gospel of John, Jesus is identified by John the Baptist as the Lamb of God. Two of John's followers then started following Jesus, intrigued by the possibility that He was Israel's long-awaited Messiah. One of them was convinced enough to seek out his brother and introduce him to the Christ.

> One of the two who heard John speak, and followed Him, was Andrew, Simon Peter's brother. He first found his own brother Simon, and said to him, "We have found the Messiah" (which is translated, the Christ). And he brought him to Jesus (John 1:40-42).

In the early days of the New Testament church, the message of the gospel resulted in the conversion of numerous individuals. Many of them were obviously influential enough to win their families as well. In many instances a family hosted a segment of the larger church in their home for worship, fellowship, and instruction.

> Now a certain woman named Lydia heard us. She was a seller of purple from the city of Thyatira, who worshiped God. The Lord opened her heart to heed the things spoken by Paul. And when she and her household were baptized, she begged us, saying, "If you have judged me to be faithful to the Lord, come to my house and stay." So she persuaded us (Acts 16:14-15).

> Greet Priscilla and Aquila, my fellow workers in Christ Jesus, who risked their own necks for my life, to whom not only I give thanks, but also all the churches of the Gentiles. Likewise greet the church that is in their house (Rom. 16:3-5).

Another area for potential lifestyle evangelism to be administered is to be found among the friends and acquaintances that we have. Work, organizations, athletic, entertainment, and other pursuits inevitably cause us to develop relationships with people whom we regularly interact. Some of them even become close friends with strong ties and lasting bonds. The believer's Christian experience should be shared and freely communicated at some point in the relationship. Committed Christians who are unashamed of their salvation and unoffensive in their expression of their Christian worldview promote the gospel and the kingdom of God.

Both the Old and New Testaments command believers to love their neighbors. A practical expression of that love would be to share a great discovery or a unique find with them. The experience of God's redemptive love is the greatest thing to which believers could introduce their neighbors. The woman at the well of Samaria was so enthused by her encounter with Jesus that she went into her town and told her neighbors about Him.

> The woman then left her waterpot, went her way
> into the city, and said to the men, "Come, see a
> Man who told me all things I ever did. Could this
> be the Christ?" . . . And many of the Samaritans
> of that city believed in Him because of the word
> of the woman who testified, "He told me all that
> I ever did" (John 4:28, 29, 39).

In the days and weeks following the experience of Pentecost, the church grew in number as the gospel message was proclaimed both publicly and privately. Luke's account in Acts reveals that in the openness of the Temple as well as in the privacy of local homes, believers shared their faith in Jesus with others. It would not be a stretch to assume that the newly converted freely talked about their decision to follow Jesus with their closest friends and acquaintances.

> So, continuing daily with one accord in the tem-
> ple, and breaking bread from house to house,
> they ate their food with gladness and simplicity
> of heart, praising God and having favor with all
> the people. And the Lord added to the church
> daily those who were being saved (Acts 2: 46-47).

Committed Christians can be effective witnesses for Christ and His church by becoming active participants in the salvation of their unsaved friends and neighbors. They should regularly pray for their redemption and look for opportunities to witness to them. They should perform acts of kindness and generosity in demonstration of brotherly love. They should invite them to events at their church which are intended to introduce unbelievers to the gospel. And they should be prepared to personally lead them to Christ.

A third area where committed Christians can be involved in lifestyle evangelism is in their local community. The local church will have a visible presence in the community, and its members should be visible as well. The local school, grocery store, shopping mall, post office, library, and a host of other places employ and serve believers who attend local churches. While they may not have full freedom to openly evangelize, they can nonetheless carry the Spirit of Christ with them into those environments. Their actions of integrity, compassion, virtue, and honesty, along with an attitude of faith, encouragement, and hope will speak volumes. We've all heard stories of people who were turned off from the church because of the un-Christian behavior of members, but what about the attractiveness of those who are truly Christlike?

> Beloved, I beg you as sojourners and pilgrims, abstain from fleshly lusts which war against the soul, having your conduct honorable among the Gentiles, that when they speak against you as evildoers, they may, by your good works which they observe, glorify God in the day of visitation (1 Pet. 2: 11-12).

> Now when they saw the boldness of Peter and John, and perceived that they were uneducated and untrained men, they marveled. And they realized that they had been with Jesus (Acts 4:13).

In addition to carrying the Spirit of Christ with them to their place of employment or into a place of business, committed Christians can do ministry in other practical ways. They can volunteer at the local hospital, nursing home, or shelter. They can represent their church by participating in family-oriented community events.

They can lead a clothing or food drive for the needy in their community. They can sign up to coach or referee games with one of the local youth sports leagues. There are numerous other opportunities for committed Christians to get out into the community and advance the kingdom of God beyond the four walls of the local church.

All that is needed is the knowledge that believers are to intentionally engage their local communities. God's plan of redemption is a work of the Spirit and is made possible through Christ, but its message is given to the believer. In that sense, we are true colaborers with God in His work of reconciling men to Himself. It is a high and holy honor for the redeemed to partner with God in the salvation of their fellowman. Through godly influence and lifestyle evangelism, committed Christians fulfill their roles in advancing the kingdom of God and promoting the church.

> But you are a chosen generation, a royal priesthood, a holy nation, His own special people, that you may proclaim the praises of Him who called you out of darkness into His marvelous light (1 Pet. 2:9).

## MEMBERSHIP ASSESSMENT

- Are you excited about your local church?
- Do you regularly invite people to visit your church?
- How often do you share your testimony with unbelievers?
- Are you involved in community activities where your light can shine?

## A FINAL CONSIDERATION

Celebrities, entertainers, and athletes are often employed to promote products or events. The more popular they may be, the more lucrative the deal or contract for their endorsement. It is surmised that their popularity and influence will increase sales and participation among the public. It is expected that they will maintain a stellar reputation, conducting themselves in a manner that enjoys public approval and does not negatively reflect upon their employers.

Once considered the darling of golf, Tiger Woods lost around $23 million in endorsement deals after reports of extramarital affairs surfaced in 2009. Companies like Gatorade, Gillette, and AT&T broke ties with Woods out of concern that their association with him would tarnish their image and hurt sales of their products. As the face and spokesman for those companies, the golfer's indiscretions would appear to have their approval if he remained. It is not uncommon for some athletic contracts to be conditioned upon not bringing the game or product into disrepute. This confirms the crucial connection between athletes/endorsers and the team or product with which they associate.

In the same manner, the committed Christian's actions will have the inevitable effect of impacting the church. Public perceptions of the church will be shaped by the committed Christians' behavior. If they have a good reputation in the community, it will bode well for the church. A bad reputation will be problematic for the church's testimony and witness. While all believers are engaged in the process of maturing as disciples of Christ, and are daily reminded of their weaknesses, the cause of the gospel will not be hindered if there is a constant dependence upon the Holy Spirit to enable us to walk worthy of our calling.

# COMMITTED CHRISTIANS DEFEND THE CHURCH

*"And they overcame him by the blood of the Lamb, and by the word of their testimony; and they did not love their lives to the death" (Rev. 12:11).*

In a bygone era, men full of zeal but lacking discernment took it upon themselves to engage in armed conflict against the perceived enemies of Christianity. It was their intention to regain biblically historical territories lost to foreign invaders who heralded a different religion, and to reestablish Christianity as the beacon of truth and righteousness. Fighting for the cause of God and in the name of God, their ventures failed because it was not approved of God. Nothing in the actions of the early church can be seen to affirm a physical and military defense of the church. A holy war cannot be won with sword and shield but must employ other means to secure God's assistance and success.

From its inception, the church of Jesus Christ has been engaged in warfare against the Enemy of God and the redeemed. Through persecution, intimidation, harassment, criticism, and other means, Satan and his forces are determined to frustrate and impede the progress of Christianity. Even though his defeat and our ultimate victory are assured, we are nonetheless encouraged to become familiar with the tactics of the Enemy and actively engage in the defense of the church. Our resistance, however, will not be after the manner of men, but by the power of the Holy Spirit. The language of the New Testament reveals that we are in a fight against spiritual forces, but our weapons are equal to the task.

> Fight the good fight of faith, lay hold on eternal life, to which you were also called (1 Tim. 6:12).

> For we do not wrestle against flesh and blood, but against principalities, against powers, against the rulers of the darkness of this age, against spiritual hosts of wickedness in the heavenly places (Eph. 6:12).

> For the weapons of our warfare are not carnal but mighty in God for pulling down strongholds, casting down arguments and every high thing that exalts itself against the knowledge of God, bringing every thought into captivity to the obedience of Christ (2 Cor. 10:4-5).

## DEFEND AGAINST OUTSIDE ATTACK

The first area of defense for the church is the most obvious, for the threat comes primarily from without. In the early church, it was seen in the disapproval of the apostles' preaching by the religious leaders. They faced imprisonment and beatings, Stephen and James were killed for the faith, and Saul of Tarsus spearheaded persecution of the Jerusalem church. But yet the church grew in number and increased in influence. Why? Because the believers did not cower in fear but faced the threat with prayer and a continued witness to the power of Christ.

In the modern era, the church is still being assaulted by forces opposed to the truth of the gospel. Believers in parts of Africa and Asia face overt persecution and worship under constant threat of violence, imprisonment, and death. Christianity is outlawed in Communist China, but a thriving church exists underground. In the West, the assault is against the historical values and practices of Christianity as an increasingly pluralistic society embraces a secular mindset. Even the American church is losing apparent ground to the onslaught of liberal philosophies and political pressure from those who do not fear God. Many in the church have sought to resist these attacks by engaging protest marches, rallies, political maneuvers, and public debate. While these efforts may have their merit, there seems to be a more biblical approach to contending against the negative forces that oppose the church.

The incident of the lame man's healing in Acts 3 ended with Peter and John being imprisoned and then threatened not to continue preaching about Jesus. What happened on their release speaks to how we should respond to the external assault on the church.

> And being let go, they went to their own companions and reported all that the chief priests and elders had said to them. So when they heard that, they raised their voice to God with one accord and said...Now, Lord, look on their threats, and grant to Your servants that with all boldness they may speak Your word, by stretching out Your hand to heal, and that signs and wonders may be done through the name of Your holy Servant Jesus. And when they had prayed, the place where they were assembled together was shaken;

> and they were all filled with the Holy Spirit, and
> they spoke the word of God with boldness. . . .
> And with great power the apostles gave witness
> to the resurrection of the Lord Jesus. And great
> grace was upon them all (Acts 4:23-24, 29-31, 33).

Three things are to be noted here: They prayed for boldness, they experienced the divine presence, and they became a powerful witness. These believers showed remarkable resolve in refusing to be intimidated by the authorities. Their actions reveal that they were more concerned about accomplishing God's will than acquiescing to men's threats. In fact, they went to God about the matter but did not question whether they should continue or alter their efforts.

1.  They prayed for boldness: Note that the specific request made by this company of believers was for courage to continue the work of ministry despite the threat of men. They did not ask for God's judgment to be meted out against the opposition; they simply asked Him to see their threats (and deal with it His way). The defensive response of the church (and the church member) to external assault is to pray that God give the believer(s) courage and fearlessness to live and serve in obedience to His will. Let God answer the attackers in the time and manner of His own choosing. Our focus must not waver from fulfilling the biblical mandate to be salt and light to the world (see Matt. 5:13-16) and carrying out the Great Commission (Matt. 28:19-20).

2.  They experienced the divine presence: In response to their request, the Holy Spirit visited the place where they were, in a manner like Pentecost. The building was shaken, and they

were given fresh empowerment to preach with boldness. When under assault from the forces of a godless society, we need to find strength in the presence of God. Through prayer and worship and with a determination to do His will, we can experience the Holy Spirit's anointing to face the challenges and overcome. Our own plans, schemes, and strength will fail us in this fight. We need the power and presence of God energizing, mobilizing, and motivating us.

3. They became a powerful witness: The believers left that prayer session full of purpose and power, and it showed in their witness. They continued to preach and proclaim the risen Christ, God confirmed their words with signs and wonders, and the church grew stronger and larger. It was obvious to all who observed them that this was more than a work of men; indeed, the grace of God was upon them. When we boldly live out our faith and allow the Holy Spirit to lead us, we can be a powerful testimony to the truth of the gospel. Hurting and bound people can experience deliverance and freedom through our actions. Fear and intimidation will cripple our witness, whereas courage and resolve will unleash the power of God in our communities.

This must be our defense against the external forces that are opposing the church today. Committed Christians must not cower at the efforts of the Enemy in their own local assembly but respond in the New Testament fashion. Partner with like-minded believers and pray for boldness, be determined to please God by obeying His Word, embrace the presence of the Holy Spirit when He answers, and go forth with power and purpose. The church did not survive and thrive through the centuries because believers yielded to the onslaught of the Enemy. It grew and progressed because they defended it against assault with more testimonies, increased witnessing, and greater power.

## DEFEND AGAINST INTERNAL DISRUPTION

The next area of defense for the church does not come from outside its walls but from within its ranks. Differing perspectives, varied opinions, and even disagreement will inevitably arise among those who comprise the body of Christ and the local committed Christians hip. After all, the church is a gathering of people from various cultures, experiences, and ethnicities bound together by the experience of salvation. It is when those differences become divisive and lead to strife and squabble that the witness of the church becomes jeopardized.

The Bible does not hide instances of disunity and discord among the followers of God. Moses' leadership was challenged on several occasions by both jealous opportunists and the impatience of the Israelites. The nation was denied entry into the Land of Promise, because fear and doubt could fester against the intentions of God. In the New Testament, the disciples of Jesus argued among themselves regarding positions in His kingdom. And the early church had to react to growing disputes between the Greek and Hebrew widows over partiality in the daily apportionment of provisions. Later, a council was convened in Jerusalem to answer demands that Gentile converts practice Jewish customs as part of their faith in Christ.

In His prayer recorded in John 17, Jesus prayed for the unity of His followers and indicated that their oneness would be a sign to the world. The Enemy of righteousness has discovered that a multifaceted attack engages the opponent from the outside and from the inside. Internal confusion, frustration, and division are very effective at retarding progress or setting the stage for self-destruction. A church that is not aware of these dangers or prepared to combat them will be mired in stagnation and lose effectiveness. Thankfully, the Scriptures also speak to the need for vigilance and action against the threat that arises from within.

As mentioned in the first chapter, the Corinthian church was plagued with numerous problems that were dividing the church and marring its witness to the wider community. The apostle Paul gave instructions to correct the attitudes and behaviors that were disrupting the life of the congregation. Among his many directives was the appeal to resist contention and maintain unity.

> Now I plead with you, brethren, by the name of our Lord Jesus Christ, that you all speak the same thing, and that there be no divisions among you, but that you be perfectly joined together in the same mind and in the same judgment. For it has been declared to me concerning you, my brethren, by those of Chloe's household, that there are contentions among you (1 Cor. 1:10-11).

In Ephesians chapter 4, Paul reminds the believers of their common experience of salvation and the consequent expression of harmony that should be evident among them. In a contemporary culture that promotes self-awareness, self-assertion, and independence, we would do well to heed these admonitions as the people of God. After all, we are members of God's family.

> I, therefore, the prisoner of the Lord, beseech you to . . . walk worthy of the calling with which you were called, with all lowliness and gentleness, with longsuffering, bearing with one another in love, endeavoring to keep the unity of the Spirit in the bond of peace. There is one body and one Spirit, just as you were called in one hope of your calling; one Lord, one faith, one baptism; one God and Father of all, who is above all, and through you all, and in you all (Eph. 4:1-6).

Love is the fruit of the Spirit, according to Galatians 5:22, and should be consistently displayed and demonstrated in the church through the believer. Where love exists, the issues that divide and disrupt can be managed and overcome. The church member should live and function with an awareness that love is not an option but a requirement for valid Christian testimony.

> This is My commandment, that you love one another as I have loved you (John 15:12).
> Let brotherly love continue (Heb. 13:1).
> We know that we have passed from death to life, because we love the brethren. He who does not love his brother abides in death (1 John 3:14).

The Epistle of James provides practical advice for the believer who wants to successfully overcome trials and the temptation to sin. It is apparent that interpersonal conflicts fueled by envy, bickering, and gossip were also prevalent enough to warrant strong admonition from the apostle. His corrective response to first-century issues is still relevant and effective for addressing twenty-first century realities.

> Where do wars and fights come from among you? Do they not come from your desires for pleasure that war in your members? . . . Therefore submit to God. Resist the devil and he will flee from you. Draw near to God and He will draw near to you...Do not speak evil of one another, brethren. He who speaks evil of a brother and judges his brother, speaks evil of the law and judges the law. But if you judge the law, you are not a doer of the law but a judge. There is one Lawgiver, who is able to save and to destroy. Who are you to judge another? (Jas. 4:1, 7, 8, 11-12).

If the advice of James is to be heeded and we are to minimize internal church conflict, then committed Christians should begin by ensuring that they are fully submitted to God. It must be a daily, continual submission that characterizes our relationship with Him. At the same time, we are commanded to resist the devil. Do not allow his tactics to seduce us into partnership with his evil intent. Deny and push back against his every attempt by refusing to accept anything less than what God requires. When we do that, we will then avoid judging or speaking evil of each other, which violates the command to love our neighbor as much as we love ourselves. The preservation of the unity and harmony of the church must be our objective in this struggle.

## DEFEND AGAINST SPIRITUAL DISEASE

The third area of concern has to do with spiritual disease. The presence of disease in the human body is identified by any condition that negatively affects normative functions. According to the English dictionary, *disease* is "an illness or disorder caused by infection, diet, condition of life or that is inherited, not by an accident."

Some diseases are classified as contagious or infectious because they can be easily passed from one person to another. Diseases are potentially dangerous because of their ability to disrupt, alter, and even bring an end to life. The response of humanity to the discovery of natural disease has been to fight, ward off, and resist it in its numerous forms.

The issue of spiritual disease is not unfamiliar to the biblical revelation. At various times God's full blessing upon His people had been withheld because of the presence of spiritual disease. Through the prophet Isaiah, God's examination of Israel's condition and consequent prognosis revealed that the nation was gravely ill. Despite their feelings to the contrary they were in rebellion against God and were in danger of divine judgment because they were a diseased people.

> Why should you be stricken again? You will revolt more and more. The whole head is sick, and the whole heart faints. From the sole of the foot even to the head, there is no soundness in it, but wounds and bruises and putrefying sores; they have not been closed or bound up or soothed with ointment (Isa. 1: 5-6).

The prophet Jeremiah drew similar conclusions in his godly pronouncements upon Judah.

> Is there no balm in Gilead, is there no physician there? Why then is there no recovery for the health of the daughter of my people? (Jer. 8:22).

> For thus says the Lord: Your affliction is incurable, your wound is severe (Jer. 30:12).

64

In the New Testament record, there is a statement about the damaging influence of sin that is allowed to go unchecked in the church. Paul likens it to leaven that permeates the dough, which lends itself to the same idea of an infectious disease that affects the body.

> Your glorying is not good. Do you not know that a little leaven leavens the whole lump? Therefore, purge out the old leaven, that you may be a new lump, since you truly are unleavened. For indeed Christ, our Passover, was sacrificed for us (1 Cor. 5: 6-7).

On the Isle of Patmos, John received revelations that were recorded for our knowledge and instruction. In particular, Jesus' review of the seven churches of Asia point to the awesome omniscience of the church's condition that He possesses. The church at Laodicea was apparently wealthy and lacking nothing materially. The economy was good, members were prospering, and life was satisfying. The same could not be said, however, about their spirituality. Among their many flaws was the disease of spiritual blindness.

> Because you say, "I am rich, have become wealthy, and have need of nothing"—and do not know that you are wretched, miserable, poor, blind, and naked—I counsel you to buy from me gold refined in the fire, that you may be rich; and white garments, that you may be clothed, that the shame of your nakedness may not be revealed; and anoint your eyes with eye salve, that you may see (Rev. 3:17-18).

How do the church and the committed Christians defend against spiritual disease in any of the forms that it may appear? Health practitioners routinely advise us that any effort to maintain good physical health must include a proper diet, appropriate rest, and plenty of exercise. After the same manner good spiritual health may be maintained by a disciplined approach that gives attention to our spiritual diet, spiritual rest, and spiritual exercise.

Our spiritual diet must consist primarily of our interaction with the Word of God. All that we know and believe about God is revealed and expressed through the revelation of Himself in the pages of Holy Scripture. His eternal purpose, perspective, plans, and His expectations of us are recorded for us to know, submit to, and partner with. For the Christian to grow in a healthy relationship with God, there must be a constant diet of the Word of God that involves reading, hearing, meditating upon, and obeying.

> But his delight is in the law of the Lord, and in His law, he meditates day and night. He shall be like a tree planted by the rivers of water, that brings forth its fruit in its season, whose leaf also shall not wither; and whatever he does shall prosper (Psalm 1:2-3).

> But He answered and said, "It is written, Man shall not live by bread alone, but by every word that proceeds from the mouth of God" (Matt. 4:4).

> As newborn babes, desire the pure milk of the word that you may grow thereby (1 Pet. 2:2).

Along with a steady diet of God's Word fueling our spiritual development, we must also take advantage of the spiritual rest that is ours as children of God. The idea of rest runs throughout the Scriptures and invariably points to cessation or settling down, reposing, or being refreshed. As believers, we are positioned to be settled down and refreshed spiritually through our relationship with Christ. Where our salvation is concerned, we are released from self-efforts at redemption and the frustration of failing to attain it. We access it by grace through faith in Christ. And where our living is concerned, we can rest from the anxieties and worries of life by resting in God's providential care.

> Come to Me, all you who labor and are heavy laden, and I will give you rest. Take My yoke upon you and learn from Me, for I am gentle and lowly in heart, and you shall find rest for your souls (Matt. 11:28-29).

In addition to a spiritual diet and spiritual rest, the believer must be engaged in spiritual exercise. Activities that build us up spiritually and keep us focused on accomplishing God's will in the earth will prevent spiritual disease. Prayer, fasting, worship, serving, and witnessing are among those disciplines that promote optimum spiritual health. Every church member should be engaged in consistent participation in these types of activities whether independently, through small groups, or as part of a churchwide effort. The best results come when one combines all three. Healthy growing churches are filled with healthy growing members who are actively engaged in spiritual exercise.

> Is this not the fast that I have chosen: to loose the bonds of wickedness, to undo the heavy burdens, to let the oppressed go free, and that you break every yoke? Is it not to share your bread with the hungry… then your light shall break forth like the morning, your health shall spring

forth speedily, and your righteousness shall go before you; the glory of the Lord shall be your rear guard (Isa. 58:6-8).

Let the word of Christ dwell in you richly in all wisdom, teaching and admonishing one another in psalms and hymns and spiritual songs, singing with grace in your hearts to the Lord (Col. 3:16).

But reject profane and old wives' fables, and exercise yourself toward godliness. For bodily exercise profits a little, but godliness is profitable for all things, having promise of the life that now is and of that which is to come (1 Tim. 4:7-8).

The defense of the church is a necessary action that every member must be involved in on some level. Acceptance into God's family also involves enlistment in God's army. The various spiritual threats from without, from within, and from disease require vigilant action. The local church can only benefit from congregants who are prepared to resist the Enemy's attempts to hinder its witness through strategic biblical responses.

## MEMBERSHIP ASSESSMENT
- Are you involved in prayer activities in and for your church?
- Are you praying for and walking in harmony with your fellow members?
- Do you regularly feed on God's Word through personal devotions and Bible reading?
- Do you fast often, witness regularly, and serve in your local church?

## A FINAL CONSIDERATION

A Florida megachurch found itself under the glare of public scrutiny, when it was reported that they failed to tip a waitress who had prepared a $735 food order from a local restaurant. The frustrated waitress had spent most of her shift preparing the order of steak and chicken dinners and did not make much in tips that day. She posted her displeasure on Facebook and went to work the next day, only to be fired for violating company policy regarding the use of social media to complain about customers.

The church had been made aware of the Facebook post and sought to make things right with the waitress. Apparently, the volunteer who picked up the meals was unaware of the policy to leave a tip. When they contacted the restaurant, it refunded the money for the order, and fired the waitress.

It was not the church's intention to have the waitress fired, according to the *Palm Beach Post*, but to tip her. They even apologized on their own Facebook page for the mishap. But now their actions had resulted in further complications for the young lady. Initial reports garnered much sympathy for the waitress and a lot of criticism for the church. Some seized the opportunity to attack the congregation about issues totally unrelated to the incident. But the church responded by reaching out to the waitress, giving her a generous tip, and offering to assist in finding employment. She was grateful to learn that several families from the church had contributed to compensate her above and beyond the normal gratuity.

This exemplifies the defensive approach that a church should take when under public attack. An act of kindness and humility goes a long way in disarming animosity and validating the Christian witness. That several families participated in making amends reveals the level of responsibility that they felt about protecting the reputation of their church in the community. They could have left the matter to the leaders but chose instead to actively participate in this benevolent mission. The external attack that resulted from failing to tip the waitress was quickly subdued through these actions that defended the church.

# Chapter 4

# COMMITTED CHRISTIANS MAINTAIN THE UNITY OF THE FELLOWSHIP

"Behold, how good and how pleasant it is for brethren to dwell together in unity!" (Psalm 133:1).

The unity of the church is to be found in our common experience of deliverance from the power of sin by the blood of Jesus Christ, and the consequent indwelling of His Holy Spirit. By its very definition, the church is comprised of those who have been called out from the world to become the family of God. Believers are tied together by their faith, their testimonies, and their practices. Irrespective of our differences in culture, language, or ethnicity, we are nonetheless undeniably linked in a fellowship of oneness.

Our Lord taught the importance of our unity as indicative of our connection with Him and for our testimony to the world. He prayed, in John 17, that our union would be like His own union with the Father: perfect, unbroken, and complete. In the previous chapter, we noted the need to defend against the danger of internal disruptions that can divide the church and

71

create discord. Here, we underscore the importance of maintaining the harmony that is expected of the church and is the wonderful experience of believers.

One of the metaphors that is used in the New Testament to describe the church is the body. In fact, the church is called the body of Christ, the Lord Jesus being the head. The human body is a wonderfully complex organism with differing parts that function together for the good of the whole. The initiatives that form in our brains are communicated via the central nervous system to the feet, arms, eyes, mouth, etc., and are executed through a harmonious interaction. A healthy body is one whose parts faithfully function according to their design and thus demonstrate a unity of purpose.

Likewise, a healthy church is one wherein all its members are functioning faithfully and cooperatively to fulfill the Lord's commands. It is characterized by uniformity of obedience to the Head and unity in the operation of the various parts. Interdependence and interconnectedness demand an understanding of partnership in the fulfillment of the various objectives of the body. Independence and renegade actions will create dysfunction and adversely affect the entire body. Therefore, unity must be pursued, achieved, and maintained.

> For as we have many members in one body, but all the members do not have the same function, so we, being many, are one body in Christ, and individually members of one another (Rom. 12:4-5).

> And if one member suffers, all the members suffer with it; or if one member is honored, all the members rejoice with it (1 Cor. 12:26).

72

In the local church, the issue of unity is extremely important for effective representation of the kingdom of God. It is also necessary for the fulfillment of the ministries of the church. Committed Christians need to be taught these truths and encouraged to do their part to ensure the unity of the fellowship. Due to the fact that our unity is revealed in our interaction with each other as members of the church, careful attention must be given to two key areas of relationship. One speaks to the issue of spiritual authority in the local church and the other relates to our love for the brethren.

## SUBMISSION TO GODLY AUTHORITY

Throughout the Scriptures it can be seen that God has established lines of authority among His people. For the Old Testament saints, He used priests, prophets, judges, and kings to give direction and instruction to Israel. In the arrangement of the New Testament church, God has established a system of authority under Christ and through the enablement of the Holy Spirit. Specific offices are identified and prescribed to give leadership to the body.

> And He Himself gave some to be apostles, some prophets, some evangelists, and some pastors and teachers, for the equipping of the saints for the work of ministry, for the edifying of the body of Christ (Eph. 4:11-12).

Various other titles have been used in the New Testament to designate those who function in ministry. Bishop, overseer, and elder are terms used by Paul and Peter in their writings to the churches of the first century. In each case they referred to those who were in positions of pastoral oversight in the church. They

73

served to instruct, guide, watch over, and build up the saints. And because of their calling to these functions those under their charge were to submit to them.

> And we urge you, brethren, to recognize those who labor among you, and are over you in the Lord and admonish you, and to esteem them very highly in love for their works sake. Be at peace among yourselves (1 Thess. 5:12-13).

> Remember those who rule over you, who have spoken the word of God to you, whose faith follow, considering the outcome of their conduct. . . . Obey those who rule over you, and be submissive, for they watch out for your souls, as those who must give account. Let them do so with joy and not with grief, for that would be unprofitable for you (Heb. 13:7, 17).

Contemporary expressions of church leadership vary according to denomination or faith tradition. Some churches are led by a group of elders, others utilize a team of pastors led by a senior or lead pastor, while many smaller churches are led by a single pastor. Each model finds justification in the New Testament account of the growth and development of the church as recorded in Acts and the Epistles. Whichever model may be practiced in a given church setting, the expectation of the members of the local assembly is to honor their leadership.

All of the ministries and functions of the local church relate to and serve under pastoral authority. The vision, direction, passion, and effectiveness of the local church are inextricably tied to the office and function of pastoral leadership. And usually, depending upon the leadership style of the local church, the highest level of spiritual authority in the local assembly is vested in the pastor or pastoral team.

Numerous incidents of pastoral and clergy abuses in various forms have created suspicion and mistrust of ministers in both society and the church. Every so often, television, print, and other media give front-page coverage to reports of scandal-plagued ministries, churches, and pastors. Although the offenders are few in comparison to the overall number of men and women engaged in pastoral ministry, the given impression is that most are dishonest. This is a grievous lie that the Enemy has successfully manipulated to his advantage to damage the image of the church in society.

It has also had the unfortunate effect of distorting the relationship between the pulpit and the pew. Some reject pastoral authority based upon past negative experiences that lead to mistrust. Others are blatantly rebellious against any pastoral authority, choosing to live, serve, and worship as they please without regard to biblical order. Like Korah, Dathan, and Abiram who challenged Moses' leadership in the wilderness (see Numbers 16), modern day church bosses assume equality with pastoral leadership and hinder the ministry and progress of the local church. Consequently, many churches are losing good pastors who leave because they have been frustrated in their attempts to lead. Chaos and confusion are inevitable in any church whose structure is out of order.

The truth is that most of the men and women engaged in pastoral and other church ministry functions are conscious of their holy calling. While cognizant of their imperfections, they are nonetheless committed to faithfully representing their faith and the kingdom of God in righteousness. They are committed to living the

Word that they proclaim to others. They are dependent upon the Holy Spirit to daily walk in a manner worthy of their calling. As such, they are to be respected, esteemed, honored, and submitted to in their respective roles of leadership. Advisory boards have their place, but the pastoral leadership is ordained by God as the highest authority in the local church.

The expectation of local committed Christians is that they demonstrate submission to the pastor. As the one ordained of God to exercise oversight in the local church, the pastor must have the willing cooperation of the membership. As the pastor faithfully ministers the Word of God through teaching and preaching, the members follow godly directives and practice obedience to the Word. As the pastor guides and manages the affairs of the church, the members work with diligently in an attitude of harmony. And when the pastor challenges behaviors and attitudes that are contrary to the Christian ideal, members accept it as godly correction and adjust themselves accordingly.

Two of Paul's associates were Timothy and Titus. He had been a spiritual father and mentor to both. They had traveled with him and discovered their own calling under his tutelage. As they took on their respective pastoral oversight and responsibilities, Paul wrote Epistles to each of them to instruct, encourage, and affirm them. He underscored the important role that they each played as leaders of God's church and challenged them to be firm, faithful, and fearless.

> You therefore, my son, be strong in the grace that is in Christ Jesus. And the things that you have heard from me among many witnesses, commit these to faithful men who will be able to teach others also (2 Tim. 2:1-2).

Preach the word! Be ready in season and out of season. Convince, rebuke, exhort, with all long-suffering and teaching (2 Tim. 4:2).

For this reason, I left you in Crete, that you should set in order the things that are lacking, and appoint elders in every city as I commanded you (Titus 1:5).

Speak these things, exhort, and rebuke with all authority. Let no one despise you (Titus 2:15).

Unity can be maintained in the local church when there is recognition and respect given by the members to the office of the pastor. As the pastor faithfully fulfills the calling as the shepherd of God's flock, the members ought to faithfully follow their pastor's leading as sheep. The harmonious interaction of this relationship answers the prayer and the expectation of Jesus, the Chief Shepherd, concerning His church. And the local church is thereby positioned for the revelation of God's power.

## LOVE FOR EACH OTHER

It stands to reason that if we have been the recipients of God's love, we should be able to love others in turn, particularly other believers. His love draws us to each other, connects us, fills us, and unites us. Like siblings, we are joined by familial ties that cause us to be committed to each other. Mutual concern, pursuits, and fidelity characterize our relationship. Even though we may differ and disagree on occasion, we nonetheless share enough commonality that we are inextricably bound together. All of this is because of God's love for us. Paul speaks to this point in his Epistle to the Ephesians.

> But God, who is rich in mercy, because of His
> great love with which He loved us, even when we
> were dead in trespasses, made us alive together
> with Christ (by grace you have been saved), and
> raised us up together, and made us sit together in
> the heavenly places in Christ Jesus. (Eph. 2:4-6)

Notice how the action of God unites us in the statement. He loved us. He made us alive together. He raised us up together. He made us sit together in heavenly places. What God has done for one of us, He has done for all of us. We are redeemed together through God's love and thus united as the body of Christ, the church. What God commands and expects concerning His church is required of all of us to fulfill just the same as we all receive His blessings. John records a specific expectation placed upon the church by the Lord Jesus Christ.

> This is My commandment, that you love one an-
> other as I have loved you. Greater love has no
> one than this, than to lay down one's life for his
> friends (John 15:12-13).

The love that we demonstrate toward each other as believers is to be patterned after Jesus' own love toward us. In fact, we see in the actions of our Lord what true love really is. It is selfless and sacrificial. It puts others and their needs first. It subdues its own concerns to address those of another. In the church, we are to have and display a love that is sacrificial. Members ought to show genuine concern and brotherhood as Christ's disciples. Against the self-awareness, self-promotion, self-assertion, and self-exaltation that prevail in our world, we must uphold the biblical standard of humility and selflessness.

One of the biblical ways that believers demonstrate sacrificial love is by sharing their resources with each other when necessary. In the weeks following Pentecost there was such a sense of unity and community that the believers made sure there was no lack among them. They willingly surrendered what possessions they could to care for each other. In so doing, the power of the Holy Spirit was revealed in both individual salvation and corporate provision.

> Now all who believed were together, and had all things in common, and sold their possessions and goods, and divided them among all, as anyone had need (Acts 2:44-45).

> Now the multitude of those who believed were of one heart and one soul; neither did anyone say that any of the things he possessed was his own, but they had all things in common . . . Nor was there anyone among them who lacked; for all who were possessors of lands or houses sold them, and brought the proceeds of the things that were sold, and laid them at the apostle's feet; and they distributed to each as anyone had need (Acts 4:32, 34-35).

What we can learn from this is not to establish some communal sect, as some have done, but rather to be aware of our brother's needs and willing to help. Charitable giving to those less fortunate is expected of a prosperous society. And while definitions of prosperity may differ from one context to the next, anytime one has something that he can help another with, he should give it. And believers should especially be predisposed towards helping other believers in need, thereby showing sacrificial love.

> By this we know love, because He laid down
> His life for us. And we also ought to lay down
> our lives for the brethren. But whoever has this
> world's goods, and sees his brother in need, and
> shuts up his heart from him, how does the love
> of God abide in him? My little children, let us
> not love in word or in tongue, but in deed and in
> truth (1 John 3:16-18).

Another characteristic of Christ's love is, it is unconditional. It is love that is motivated by the sovereign decision of the giver, not the merit of the recipient. God does not love us because we deserve His love; rather He loves us despite our unworthiness of His love. We can do nothing to earn or to eliminate His love for us. The wonder of His love is that it is freely given to those who ought to receive His wrath and judgment. It is the highest form and expression of love. It is almost incomprehensible but for the fact that we surmise that God loves us, not for who we are, but for who we can become. The Scriptures intimate this in its description of a God and Savior who bestow love on an unworthy humanity.

> The Lord has appeared of old to me saying: "Yes,
> I have loved you with an everlasting love; There-
> fore with lovingkindness I have drawn you"
> (Jer. 31:3).

> For God so loved the world that He gave His
> only begotten Son, that whoever believes in Him
> should not perish but have everlasting life (John
> 3:16).

> But God demonstrates His own love toward us,
> in that while we were still sinners, Christ died for
> us (Rom. 5:8).

Our love for each other as brethren must be characterized as unconditional if we are to love as Christ commands. We must love each other without reservation, partiality, or hypocrisy. To do that, we must unlearn the world's way of loving others based upon their suitability or acceptability. Instead, we must look beyond imperfections, because we're all imperfect people anyway, and see each other as God sees us— in need of unconditional love. In the manner that God loves us, we are to love each other. The love of the believer must therefore be in spite of, not because of. The best that we can become must be deemed more valuable than the worst that we are.

In the local church this is demonstrated in patience, genuine concern, and impartiality among brethren. Committed Christians must show unconditional love by being willing to forgive offenses, pursuing reconciliation when wronged, and promoting peace instead of discord. They must be prepared to allow for differences with their brothers while clinging to the common bond that unites God's family. And since this kind of love is the fruit of the Spirit, they must rely upon God's love to radiate through him. In so doing, they will display the kind and quality of love that Paul, Peter, and John encouraged believers to possess.

> Love suffers long and is kind; love does not envy; love does not parade itself, is not puffed up; does not behave rudely, does not seek its own, is not provoked, thinks no evil; does not rejoice in iniquity, but rejoices in the truth; bears all things, believes all things, hopes all things, endures all things (1 Cor. 13:4-7).

> Let love be without hypocrisy. Abhor what is evil. Cling to what is good. Be kindly affectionate to one another with brotherly love, in honor giving preference to one another (Rom. 12:9-10).

> Above all things have fervent love for one another, for "love will cover a multitude of sins" (1 Pet. 4:8).

> Beloved, let us love one another, for love is of God; and everyone who loves is born of God and knows God. He who does not love does not know God, for God is love…Beloved, if God so loved us, we also ought to love one another (1 John 4:7-8, 11).

The unity of the local church will be maintained through the willful participation of committed Christians. With the understanding that our unity has been prayed for and anticipated by Christ, we should be predisposed to experiencing it in our churches. Our relationships with our leaders and with each other will determine the level of our commitment to it. Let us not allow the tactics of the Enemy or our own human frailties to pull us apart from each other. Instead, let us demonstrate that we are truly one: in faith, in hope, and in charity.

## MEMBERSHIP ASSESSMENT

- Are you submitted to the God-ordained authority in your church?
- Do you believe that your pastor has been assigned by God to minister to you?
- In what ways do you show concern for your brethren?
- Are you patient and forgiving towards those who wrong you?
- Is your love for your brethren unconditional?

## A FINAL CONSIDERATION

Several studies have revealed that the mighty elephant is no match for a tiny ant. The online magazine *Smithsonian* reported on the findings of biologists who studied a species of the African acacia tree that has a symbiotic relationship with ants. The tree provides shelter and food for the ants, who in turn ward off hungry elephants who can potentially destroy the tree.

It appears that elephants are very sensitive on the underside of their trunks, and the prospect of being bitten by angry ants is not worth a meal of that species of tree. The ants have been known to swarm to any part of the tree that is being disturbed, hence elephants will move away quickly if they smell their presence.

These ants provide a fitting example of the power and necessity of unity. Their existence and way of life depends upon the tree, and they will come together to protect it. The importance of the church to the believer cannot be overstated. Local churches play an instrumental role in Christian formation and development. We were designed to grow through fellowship and community. We function best within the context of relationships with others. When members appreciate the local church for what it represents to their lives, they will strive to maintain its unity.

Chapter 5

# COMMITTED CHRISTIANS HONOR AND SUPPORT CHURCH LEADERSHIP

"Receive him therefore in the Lord with all gladness, and
hold such men in esteem" (Phil. 2:29).

In the previous chapter, we established the significance of the pastoral function and office to the kingdom of God, especially the local church. It is one of the five ministry gifts that Christ has given to His church (Ephesians 4:11) for the purpose of bringing it to maturity. And because the pastoral function is likened to that of a shepherd, the pastor is in the unique position of being the leader of the local church. It is his responsibility to lead God's flock to the green pastures and cool waters of God's Word and the Christian walk that will enable spiritual growth and development to occur. And because we customarily honor those whose efforts benefit others, we are to honor, respect, and esteem the pastor.

Numerous instances and verses in the Scripture encourage, reflect, or command the honoring of God's chosen ones who serve His people. In the Old Testament, the priests were to be given special distinction because of their unique service as the intermediaries between God and man. The institution of their function (Exodus 29) was prescribed by God and included careful details and much ceremony, all of which set them apart from their brethren. In the time of the judges, Jephthah and Deborah were both esteemed enough to be sought out by their countrymen for leadership and guidance in times of national turmoil. And the prophet Elijah was fed in a time of famine by a widow who honored him as the spokesman of God. In that instance, her meager supplies were miraculously multiplied because she had faith in his word.

In the New Testament, those who served in pastoral capacities and gave leadership to the church were treated with honor. Both the actions of the people and the encouragement of the apostolic writers affirm the need to esteem godly leadership. In Acts 10, Peter is summoned to Caesarea to meet with a group of Gentiles who are worshipers of God. This divine assignment is orchestrated by the Holy Spirit who works to bring both parties together. Upon meeting Peter, Cornelius, a centurion of the Italian Regiment, prostrates himself before the apostle in an act of high regard.

> As Peter was coming in, Cornelius met him and fell down at his feet and worshiped him. But Peter lifted him up, saying, "Stand up; I myself am also a man" (Acts 10:25-26).

In Galatians 4, Paul reminds the brethren of how they had treated him during his time among them. At the time, he was plagued by an obvious infirmity that may have been caused by his labor among them. It was such that they could have disregarded his message and refused to hear him. They did no such thing, but rather received him as they would have received Jesus himself. They were hospitable and respectful toward the apostle.

> You know that because of physical infirmity I preached the gospel to you at the first. And my trial which was in my flesh you did not despise or reject, but you received me as an angel of God, even as Christ Jesus (Gal. 4:13-14).

In his third Epistle, John addressed a situation that was occurring at one of the churches under his apostolic oversight. An overly ambitious and arrogant individual by the name of Diotrephes resisted the apostle's authority, spoke ill of him, and led others to reject any persons sent by the apostle to the church. Whether Diotrephes was himself a leader is not clear from the text, but what is certain is, he acted dishonorably toward one of Jesus' original disciples who had obvious authority over him and created an unhealthy atmosphere in the church. John's response is a promise to publicly reprimand Diotrephes when he visits the church, and to encourage the believers to follow good examples while rejecting evil ones. His reaction makes it clear that dishonoring God's leaders should not be tolerated in the church.

> I wrote to the church, but Diotrephes, who loves to have the preeminence among them, does not receive us. Therefore, if I come, I will call to mind his deeds which he does, prating against us with malicious words. And not content with that, he himself does not receive the brethren, and forbids those who wish to, putting them out of the church. Beloved, do not imitate what is evil, but what is good. He who does good is of God, but he who does evil has not seen God (3 John 9-11).

In the local church, it is expected that the pastor will be given honor and respect as God's chosen leader. The position that he holds is such that he should be held in high regard. Prime ministers, presidents, sovereign leaders and other heads of state are given honor and distinction among men. Their influence and authority, however, is confined to the realm of men. Pastors, on the other hand, wield influence both on earth and in heaven. They are the ones who have the responsibility to communicate the truths of God's kingdom to believers, who in turn live out those truths in the earth. They, by virtue of their calling and position, regularly navigate between the realities of the natural realm and the revelations of the spiritual realm.

The work of the pastor in the local church is arguably more significant than the work of other earthly leaders. The efforts of the pastoral office hold implications and ramifications that will outlast this life and extend into eternity. Through the ministry of the pastor, committed Christians and congregants are prepared for eternal existence. The labor of political, social, or governmental leaders can only affect this life. Their efforts are directed toward and hold benefit for our temporal existence alone. Hence, the call of God to the pastoral ministry is a high and holy calling that demands humility, diligence, and faithfulness on the part of the called. But, it also demands submission, respect, and honor among those the pastor serves.

> Let the elders who rule well be counted worthy of double honor, especially those who labor in the word and doctrine (1 Tim. 5:17).

In addition to admonitions to honor and respect the pastor, the Scriptures also direct those who are benefitted by his function to support him economically. The work and service of the pastor to the church is to be underwritten by the generosity and faithful giving of the congregation. It is the desire and design of God that those whose primary labor is the ministerial duties of the church and Kingdom derive temporal benefit from the church in return. Again, this was established in the Old Testament priestly system where God instructed that a portion of the offerings and sacrifices were to be given to the priests. Upon their entry to the Promised Land, they were denied any share in the tribal allotment of Canaan but instead promised support from the people.

> Then the Lord said to Aaron: "You shall have no inheritance in their land, nor shall you have any portion among them; I am your portion and your inheritance among the children of Israel. Behold, I have given the children of Levi all the tithes in Israel as an inheritance in return for the work which they perform, the work of the tabernacle of meeting" (Num. 18:20-21).

> And this shall be the priest's due from the people, from those who offer a sacrifice, whether it is bull or sheep: they shall give to the priest the shoulder, the cheeks, and the stomach. The first fruits of your grain and your new wine and your oil, and the first of the fleece of your sheep, you shall give him. For the Lord your God has chosen him out of all your tribes to stand to minister in the name of the Lord, him and his sons forever (Deut. 18:3-5).

In the New Testament, the Lord Jesus prescribed that His disciples should be supported by those to whom they ministered. Both Matthew and Luke record the sending forth of the disciples (twelve in Matthew and seventy in Luke) with specific instructions to take no provisions for themselves. They were to anticipate and accept the hospitality offered to them by those who were willing to receive their ministry.

> Provide neither gold nor silver nor copper in your money belts, nor bag for your journey, nor two tunics, nor sandals, nor staffs; for a worker is worthy of his food (Matt. 10:9-10).

> And remain in the same house, eating and drinking such things as they give, for the laborer is worthy of his wages. Do not go from house to house (Luke 10:7).

In his first letter to the Corinthians, Paul argues that it is appropriate for churches to care for their pastors. In the ninth chapter, he points out that the soldier, the farmer, and the shepherd are rightfully given some form of payment for their service. He further reasoned that it was normal and customary for laborers who worked hard at planting and cultivating the crop to receive a share in the harvest. And even the ox was not to be denied the opportunity to feed while treading the grain.

> Do you not know that those who minister the holy things eat of the things of the temple, and those who serve at the altar partake of the offerings of the altar? Even so the Lord has commanded that those who preach the gospel should live from the gospel (1 Cor. 9:13-14).

Again, it is worth noting that clergy abuses in finances and prosperity preaching have served to discredit the notion that the church should support its pastors financially. Some high-profile ministers with megachurches and celebrity status are notorious for demanding exorbitant fees for preaching engagements. Others have manipulated people into giving large sums of money while expecting a financial blessing from the Lord in return. There have even been instances where audiences have been encouraged to give money in return for a personal prophetic word from someone claiming to have the gift of prophecy.

It is regrettable that some have made profit and material gain their motivation and message in the church. God will deal with those who have perverted their call and ministry, and we should exercise good judgment and discernment regarding questionable teachings and practices. It does not, however, abrogate the fact that the Scriptures direct the church to underwrite the financial support of the minister.

The wayward sons of Eli, Hophni, and Phinehas, perverted their priestly functions by taking advantage of the people and satisfying their lusts, but God dealt with them in His time and in His way. The priestly responsibilities and privileges were not altered or revised because of their bad practices, however. The perspective of the Scripture is that these were rogue individuals who suffered the judgment of God for their behavior. In the same way, the actions of some in the ministry should not be allowed to detract from what God has ordained in His Word.

> If we have sown spiritual things for you, is it a great thing if we reap your material things? (1 Cor. 9:11).

91

> Let him who is taught the word share in all good
> things with him who teaches. (Gal. 6:6)

The support of the church for the pastor goes beyond that of taking care of his financial needs. The work of ministry is tedious and exacting. Pastors, though called and anointed to function in their office, are subject to weariness and exhaustion from the intense nature of their duties. Giving leadership, guidance, instruction, and service to the church, along with the varying nuances of interacting with the congregants through worship and fellowship, is no walk in the park. Pastors must constantly battle against discouragement and burnout in the course of ministry. And they must have vigilant people around them who are ready to assist them in a time of need.

This is demonstrated by the occasion of Israel's battle with Amalek as recorded in Exodus 17:8-13. While the weary nation camped in the valley of Rephidim, they were accosted by the hostile Amalekites and forced to defend themselves. The strategy of Moses was to send Joshua with men to engage the enemy while he ascended the hill overlooking the valley to intercede during the conflict. Aaron and Hur accompanied Moses, and their actions reveal why pastors need people around them who are sensitive to their needs.

> And so it was, when Moses held up his hand, that
> Israel prevailed; and when he let down his hand,
> Amalek prevailed. But Moses' hands became
> heavy; so they took a stone and put it under him,
> and he sat on it. And Aaron and Hur supported
> his hands, one on one side, and the other on the
> other side; and his hands were steady until the go-
> ing down of the sun. So Joshua defeated Amalek

and his people with the edge of the sword (Exod.
17:11-13).

Though the battle was raging in the plain below
them, Aaron and Hur were observant enough to notice
that the outcome of this conflict was directly connected
to their leader. Moses was not up there just to watch, but
he involved himself with the lifting of his hands. Aaron
and Hur took their cue and looked for an opportunity
to assist. The fight was no doubt intense and lengthy,
and they saw their leader struggling to keep his hands
raised. They were concerned enough to help him, and
innovative enough to devise the plan of seating him on
a rock and then holding up Moses' hands.

Several things can be learned here. First, every pastor
needs someone who will stand with him in ministry,
and particularly in times of spiritual conflict. Committed
Christians should be willing to partner with the pastor
by supporting and giving assistance when necessary.
Second, the church member should be conscious of the
pastor's need to rest and recuperate in the course of
ministry. Members should make sure that their pastor
regularly takes a real vacation (away from ministry), as
well as regular times of physical and emotional renewal.
Third, as Aaron and Hur came alongside Moses to hold
up his hands, committed Christians should be prepared
to supply strength to their pastor. Finding ways to ease
the burden of what is done in ministry may call for one
to be an armorbearer, water carrier, or chauffeur to the
pastor.

The significance of the two men's actions cannot be
ignored. What would have happened if Aaron and Hur
had not been there with Moses? How different would
the outcome of the battle and the recorded incident

have been? Moses was grateful for the intervention of these ready and willing men. Indeed, the warriors on the field, as well as the nation at large, owed them a debt of gratitude. But it could be argued that these men were there with Moses, not just because he had invited them to come; but they were there by God's design to play their necessary role in the assistance of their leader. In the same manner, committed Christians are not there to just receive ministry and blessing from the service of their pastor; they have been assigned there to partner with and be a blessing to their pastor as well.

Another way that congregations can demonstrate support is by regularly praying for their pastor. The nature of pastoral ministry is such that the individual is a constant target for spiritual assault. If the shepherd is smitten, the sheep may scatter. If the pastor is brought down or falls, it results in confusion and disillusionment in the congregation. Some weak persons may even turn away from the church and God. Unbelievers and those who are opposed to the church use it to justify their positions. Satan delights in wreaking this kind of havoc in the body of Christ.

In Acts chapter 12, King Herod launched an offensive against the church by having James, the brother of John, beheaded. It was a bold strike against the apostles and followers of Jesus that gave pleasure to the Jewish opposition of the church. What religious persecution had failed to accomplish (Acts 6), they now hoped political persecution would make possible. The suppression of Christ's influence through the preaching of His gospel and growth of the church was their desire. Herod's next act was to have Peter arrested and imprisoned with the intent to kill him as well. What he did not anticipate was the resilience of the church that sprang into action by interceding for the beloved apostle.

> Peter was therefore kept in prison, but constant prayer was offered to God for him by the church. . . . Now behold, an angel of the Lord stood by him, and a light shone in the prison; and he struck Peter on the side and raised him up, saying, "Arise quickly!" And his chains fell off his hands (Acts 12:5, 7).

The prayerful intervention of the believers enabled Peter to escape Herod's evil intentions. What if they had not prayed? Might he not have suffered the same fate as James? In the same way, Satan has devised various schemes to bring down the pastor, and it is incumbent upon the committed Christians hip to constantly cover their leader in prayer. Pray that God shields the pastor and the pastoral family from Satanic onslaught. Pray that the pastor remains committed to being led by the Holy Spirit in both life and ministry. Pray that the pastor never deviates from or compromises the truth of the gospel. Both the work and mission are too significant to take for granted, and the church must develop the habit of praying for the pastor.

Paul consistently requested the prayers of the congregations to whom he ministered. He had developed enough of a relationship with the believers in the various regions that he could anticipate their supplications on his behalf. He had worked with them, helped establish them, and given them pastoral oversight. The challenges of his ministry were such that he needed a covering of prayer from those who had benefitted from his preaching. They could authenticate his calling and verify the anointing of God upon his life. They would be interested in his continued success. They were the right ones to intercede, supplicate, and petition God on his behalf.

> Now I beg you, brethren, through the Lord Jesus Christ, and through the love of the Spirit, that you strive together with me in prayers to God for me, that I may be delivered from those in Judea who do not believe, and that my service for Jerusalem may be acceptable to the saints (Rom. 15:30-31).

> [Pray] for me, that utterance may be given to me, that I may open my mouth boldly to make known the mystery of the gospel (Eph. 6:19).

Good committed Christians support their church and pastor. They honor their leader as God's assigned shepherd for their spiritual growth. They esteem and respect their pastor for the holy office and function. The pastor is appreciated for the gifts and calling. Believers find ways to stand with and refresh their pastor. They realize they are there to partner with their leader in ministry. They ensure their pastor's temporal needs are taken care of by faithfully giving. They initiate and participate in efforts to be a blessing to their pastor financially. They pray regularly for their pastor and family. They intercede on behalf of their pastor during times of challenge and difficulty in the church. In all this, committed Christians honor and support their pastor in accordance with the instruction and example of the Scriptures.

## MEMBERSHIP ASSESSMENT

- In what ways do you honor your pastor?
- Are you familiar with your church's approach to compensating your pastor?
- Do you practice giving or doing something extra for your pastor?
- Do you regularly pray for your pastor and family?
- How can you be an Aaron or a Hur to your pastor?

## A FINAL CONSIDERATION

Margaret Feinberg is a writer and speaker from Utah. One October, for Clergy Appreciation Month, she solicited feedback from pastors regarding meaningful expressions of appreciation their members had given. Here is one response reported on her blog:

*Every weekend—really everyday—I am encouraged by my congregation. After each service, I'm stunned by their life-giving words. It's not that they dole out mere compliments. They aren't simply saying, "Nice sermon, Pastor" as they walk out the door. They say things like, "My life is being changed, and here's why…" "My marriage is being transformed, and we want you to know what God is doing…" It's stories of life-change—not mere compliments—that inspire me to continue to throw myself into ministry. My church keeps me from ever wondering if "my labor is in vain."*

*My church is also very thoughtful. They listen to the things I share about my life or family in my messages, and they give meaningful gifts they know will really bless us. Last week, one individual in our church wrote me a beautiful thank you note and enclosed a gift card to one of my favorite bakeries. Another woman (whose whole family is being transformed by Jesus) baked me some of her gourmet choc-olate chip cookies. These are thoughtful, inexpensive ways to show you care about your pastor (They are not, however, helping my diet).*

*Perhaps the greatest example of appreciation happened when I met some friends for dinner. Little did I know that they had other plans for us that evening. When we arrived at the restaurant to meet our friends, we were picked up in a limo and brought to the house of one of my board members. Their backyard was beautifully decorated, and a live band was performing. My family, my staff, and all their families were then treated to a multicourse gourmet meal, prepared and served by dozens of volunteers from our church. Our younger children were entertained by a dear friend who is a preschool teacher, and our older kids were treated to a night on the town in the limousine with some incredible church friends. It was such an honor and a delight to have—not just my family—but the family of my whole team honored by our church. I will never forget that night!*

*Here's the truth about church ministry: Nobody's get-ting rich . . . but nobody cares about being rich. We're rich in love and friendship in this incredible community we get to pastor. Because of the fierce love of my church, I walk away most weekends exclaiming, "I can't believe I get to do this!"*

There are many more vivid examples of congrega-tional support and appreciation for pastoral leadership. They, along with this one, reveal the powerful impact of the mutual ministry that exists between the pastor and the member. The cause of the kingdom of God is greatly advanced when this is a characteristic of the lo-cal church.

Chapter 6

# COMMITTED CHRISTIANS WORK IN HARMONY WITH THE LOCAL CHURCH

"And I told them of the hand of my God which had been
good upon me, and also of the king's words that he had
spoken to me. So they said, "Let us rise up and build."
Then they set their hands to this good work"
(Neh. 2:18).

T he mission and work of the church has been established by the Lord Jesus in the instructions
He gave to His disciples. Most notably, the Great
Commission outlines the general scope of activity that
should be performed by the church at large. The message of the gospel is clear and undeniable, but how each
local expression of the church will proclaim the message
and fulfill the mandate will vary depending upon the
culture, geographical location, or other considerations.
The peculiar specifics of each congregation's method of
ministry will be based upon the vision of that church.
Founded upon the Word of God and intended to fulfill
Christ's commands, the local church vision will give direction to all of its ministerial activity.

The importance of a vision cannot be overstated. It is a necessity for the maximum productivity of the local church. There must be a clear sense of direction for ministry efforts and a discernible path to achieving the objectives. Congregations that exist without a clear sense of purpose and direction will soon find themselves trying to do everything while accomplishing nothing. A definite vision for the local church will clarify misconceptions, focus endeavors, and validate achievements. Members will be able to know where they are going, how to get there, and when they have arrived. All the various gifts and talents of the congregation will be used toward the realization of the vision.

The Scripture indicates that the absence of vision is counterproductive. Without a guiding sense of purpose, people tend to follow their own minds. In a church setting, this can be disastrous. What programs will be implemented? Where will ministry efforts be focused? How will funds be spent? These and other questions will plague the visionless, purposeless church.

> Where there is no vision, the people are unre-
> strained, but happy is he who keeps the law
> (Prov. 29:18).

The establishment of the local church vision will usually come through the pastoral leadership of the church. In the Scripture, vision was usually given to one individual who in turn communicated it to others. For example, the vision to build the ark was given to Noah, and his family followed along. Also, the vision to free Israel from Egypt's bondage was given first to Moses, who then informed Israel and Pharaoh of God's intentions. And the prophet Habakkuk was given a divine directive that was to be published among the people.

> Then the Lord answered me and said: "Write the
> vision and make it plain upon tablets, that he
> may run who reads it" (Hab. 2:2).

Even in the New Testament, the pattern can be discerned both in the behavior of the early church and in the writings of the apostles. The argument that converted Gentiles should be circumcised was resisted in testimonies from Peter, Barnabas, and Paul in Acts 15, but it is James who renders the decision that is accepted and publicized throughout the churches. Later in his ministry, Paul was given a vision that pointed those traveling with him to a specific area for ministry. Further, his instructions to Titus and Timothy set the tone for doctrinal beliefs and ministerial practices in the churches under their watch. And the Revelation message of Jesus through John to the churches of Asia is addressed to the pastors of those churches. In today's church, it may be necessary for the pastor to be assisted by the ministers or elders who serve along with him, or even the congregation, in determining the vision. He, however, should take the lead in the process.

## AGREEMENT WITH THE VISION

Once the vision has been determined and established through the initiative of the local church pastor or pastoral team, committed Christians are to come into agreement with that vision. They are to demonstrate an acceptance of the focus and direction of the ministry as determined through the vision process. By so doing, they acknowledge that the vision represents God's will for that local assembly. They say yes to the divine purpose that drives the local church's efforts in ministering the gospel, representing the kingdom of God, and edifying believers. Their attitudes are to be compliance and cooperation with the proclaimed vision of the church.

The experience of Nehemiah in his efforts to rebuild Jerusalem's walls with the assistance of the citizens of the city speaks clearly to the issue of agreement with the vision. While this account is not of a pastor and his members, the principles derived from the cooperation of the cupbearer and his fellow countrymen are applicable to the church context. In the first chapter of the book bearing his name, Nehemiah learns of the distressing state of his people.

Though he held a comfortable position in the palace of Persia's ruler, he was burdened by the news of Jerusalem's state and driven to prayer and fasting. It is in this time of prayer and supplication that he develops a vision to see Jerusalem's walls rebuilt and hope restored to his people. In the second chapter, he gains the support and encouragement of the king to make the journey and carry out the plan. Upon arriving, he assesses the situation; and after three days, he assembles the rulers and elders of the people to share his vision.

> Then I said to them, "You see the distress that we are in, how Jerusalem lies waste, and its gates are burned with fire. Come and let us build the wall of Jerusalem, that we may no longer be a reproach." And I told them of the hand of my God which had been good upon me, and also of the king's words that he had spoken to me. So they said, "Let us rise up and build." Then they set their hands to this good work (Neh. 2:17-18).

The response of the rulers and elders to Nehemiah's vision is agreement and acceptance. His words were encouraging and filled with passion. His testimony convinced them. The support of the king lent authenticity to his mission. Plus, the outlining of his vision was inspirational enough for them to get behind it immediately.

Please note several things from this incident. First, the argument could have been made that Nehemiah was an outsider. He served in the court of Persia; whereas, these people lived in Jerusalem. Why should they be bothered to support his dream? The truth is that though the people lived in the city, none of them had developed the vision to rebuild its walls. Perhaps discouragement and apathy had set in and they were resigned to their conditions. It was Nehemiah alone who possessed the passion and the plan to address the situation. Consequently, no objection was offered from the rulers and elders to Nehemiah's plan.

Second, the vision of Nehemiah moved the king of Persia to action. It secured his interest and investment. There was an undeniable sense of God's providence in the initiative, and Nehemiah masterfully conveyed it to the elders. No doubt they recognized the truth of his words and were seized with hope and expectation. The potential and possibilities of rebuilding were hard to ignore or dismiss. They had caught a glimpse of the future in that moment, and they were filled with a desire for what they had seen.

Third, they gave both verbal and physical assent to the proclaimed vision. The spoken consensus was that they should *"rise up and build."* But more than just talking about it, they *"set their hands"* to the task. They began to make the necessary preparations to fulfill the vision of rebuilding the walls. It is easy to say yes to good ideas and plans, but it is impossible to show commitment to them without taking action. There must be a connection between what you say and what you do. Agreement with the vision will always be seen in the combined movement of the head, the heart, and the hands.

## ALIGNMENT WITH THE VISION

Beyond revealing agreement with the vision of the local church, committed Christians must also be prepared to come into alignment with the stated vision. This refers to demonstrating acceptance of the church's focus by seeking out ways to help. What role can they play? Where do members fit within the mission of the church? How can their particular gifts enhance the ministry's efforts? Again, we look to the inspiration of Nehemiah's vision upon the people's efforts to rebuild Jerusalem's walls.

The third chapter of Nehemiah lists the names of the men and various groups who participated in the rebuilding effort. Included among the group are Eliashib, the high priest, the individual priests, the Levites, and others. They all took on sections of the project and put their hands to the work that needed to be done. In fact, there was such a sense of personal responsibility for the project that certain groups or individuals focused their efforts specifically on those areas closest to them.

> Beyond the Horse Gate, the priests made repairs, each in front of his own house. After them Zadok the son of Immer made repairs in front of his own house. After him Shemaiah the son of Shechaniah, the keeper of the East Gate, made repairs (Neh. 3:28-29).

The fact that these and others chose to work on those sections immediately in front of their homes demonstrates that they were completely aligned with Nehemiah's vision. They did not sit back and wait for others to do what was clearly within their own power to accomplish. They took ownership of the vision by becoming involved at the point where the vision came closest to them. A broken-down section of the wall right outside their front doors meant that they would be vulnerable to attack. It would be in their best interest to work at securing those sections where they lived.

The record of Nehemiah relates that the entire effort was so well-supported that they soon had the wall rebuilt up to one half its height. The reason given for the enthusiastic support and quick success was that the "people had a mind to work" (4:6). Their hearts were wholly given to the rebuilding effort. They had not only agreed with the vision of Nehemiah, they had also aligned themselves with the vision. Each individual and family had found a place in the project and lent their assistance to its fulfillment. Their actions instruct us as to how effectively a vision can be realized when each person takes ownership of it by coming into alignment with it.

In the local church, committed Christians must be determined to find out how they can help to accomplish the vision. They must discover ways in which their unique gifts and abilities can be used toward its fulfillment. They must take ownership of the vision by working hard in those areas or aspects of the vision that are closest to their interests. They must put their whole hearts and minds into the corporate effort, knowing that their roles are vital to the overall success of the church. When they find their place in the vision and develop a mind to work, the local church will make great strides toward successful ministry.

## ASSIGNMENT WITH THE VISION

Assignment with the vision involves acknowledging that it is a God-given directive for the local church. It is His divine instruction for that specific group of believers that together form part of the larger body of Christ. It is their assigned duty or set of tasks that connect them to the overall mission of the Christian church. It is recognizing that the vision represents God's call upon that local ministry. Agreement with the vision states, "This is the vision." Alignment with the vision proclaims, "This is where I fit in this vision." And assignment with the vision concludes, "This is God's work."

An account from Paul's second missionary journey in the New Testament will serve to underscore the significance of agreement, alignment, and this third aspect of assignment with the vision. In Acts 16:6-8, Paul is traveling with Silas, Timothy, Luke, and possibly others as they attempt to take the gospel into parts of Asia. They acknowledge the hand of the Holy Spirit in their efforts by noting that He forbade and would not allow them to go into certain areas. A clear sense of direction came to them, however, through a vision that Paul received in the night.

> And a vision appeared to Paul in the night. A man of Macedonia stood and pleaded with him, saying, "Come over to Macedonia and help us." Now after he had seen the vision, immediately we sought to go to Macedonia, concluding that the Lord had called us to preach the gospel to them (Acts 16:9-10).

106

In this instance, Paul's vision was a direct revelation from God. It was not the indirect type of vision, sensed and grasped through prayer and faith, which is the subject of this chapter. The incident is nonetheless instructive to the local church context where the will of God, directly or indirectly revealed, is to be pursued by the congregation. First, note that there was no doubting that Paul had received the vision. The group had spent enough time with him to know his passion for ministry and sensitivity to the Holy Spirit. He was the obvious leader of the mission and had earned their trust. That God would select him to be the recipient of the vision would raise no questions among them. And they were convinced of what he told them, because they were convinced of who he was. Consequently, there was wholehearted agreement with the vision.

Second, the group came into strict alignment with Paul's vision. Though they may each have had ideas about where they should take the gospel, they forsook them to give priority to what Paul related to them. Without debate or delay, the company of missionary evangelists turned their efforts to traveling to Macedonia. A sense of urgency in their actions revealed their eagerness to fulfill the vision. It can be seen that they literally took ownership of the vision by the statement, *"we sought to go into Macedonia."* Paul may have been the recipient of the vision, but it was for all of them to pursue.

Third, the missionary group viewed the vision as their assignment from God. As Paul related the details of the vision to them, they became convinced that God was sending them a clear message. They had been prevented by the Holy Spirit from venturing to other areas and were anxious to know where He was leading. The answer was unmistakable in the plea for help coming from the citizen of Macedonia. God had spoken, and they were ready to comply. Luke records that they all drew the conclusion *"that the Lord had called us to preach the gospel to them."* Their perspective was that the vision was something more than an objective. It was, in fact, their mission and their assignment.

The committed Christians must demonstrate an understanding of assignment regarding the vision of the local church. They must view it as God's directive for the ministry. Therefore, it becomes more than a suggested route or plan of action; it is a divinely ordained strategy for the fulfillment of God's purposes for that local church. It is a corporate assignment that demands the agreement and alignment of those who comprise that church. Personal preferences, desires, and agendas must give way to the priority of the vision. Through harmonious effort, the members of the church must take the responsibility for and strive toward the fulfillment of the vision. By doing so, they answer a resounding yes to the call of God upon that local ministry and help it to accomplish its destiny.

## MEMBERSHIP ASSESSMENT
- Are you familiar with the vision of your church?
- Do you see the vision as God's directive for your local church?
- In what ways do you demonstrate agreement and alignment with the vision?
- Are you fully committed to seeing the vision become a reality?

## A FINAL CONSIDERATION

The mission statement of Granger Community Church, in Indiana, is "Helping people take their next steps toward Christ . . . together." The thriving church that had begun in the founding pastor's living room in the mid-1980s, found itself stagnated after twenty years of steady growth. The progress of the past was threatened by challenges in communication and leadership, and decline began to occur.

Two significant actions enabled the church to refocus and regain momentum. At a leadership retreat led by the pastor, a new vision for the church emerged as the staff sought God for direction. The group left convinced that God wanted them to focus on becoming *missional* and *attractional*. The leaders then polled their church and community for a sense of God's leading. The combined results led to the creation of a vision that emphasized being the church in the community and measuring success by the impact of its presence outside the walls of the church building.

The new focus ignited a fire among the congregation as members passionately participated in pursuing the vision. According to an article in *Outreach Magazine*, "Part of this vision involves the launch of missional communities where people plant small congregations in their neighborhood or domain of society. . . . These communities range from a businessman who works 60 hours a week, but finds time to lead business partners and associates each week to a group who works at an inner-city soup kitchen."

Numerous individuals have been converted and added to the church through this approach in the years since. Growth has become so dynamic that Granger now has a second location in Elkhart, Indiana. The thriving church continues its emphasis on serving the community with a missional focus, demonstrating the power of corporate vision.

Chapter 7

# COMMITTED CHRISTIANS SERVE FOR THE GLORY OF GOD

"And whatever you do, do it heartily, as to the Lord and
not to men" (Col. 3:23).

The Scriptures are quite clear in pointing out that God expects men and women to serve Him. He has created us and given us life and He reigns over all of His creation. The functions of nature operate according to His dictates and design. With unfailing regularity, the sun rises and sets each day, the seasons change in uniform order, and time passes in weeks, months, and years. Scientists are yet discovering how remarkably systematic and structured the various forms of life seem to be on planet Earth. All this points to God's orderly establishment of nature and the laws that govern its existence.

Mankind has been declared to be God's highest work in creation. Whereas He spoke other creatures into existence, He put His hands and His breath into the origin of man. And while other creatures function on the level of instinct and impulse, man alone was given the attributes of personality, reason, and free will. It is precisely by his ability to freely choose his actions that man caused the world to be infested with sin and stand in need of redemption. Instead of choosing to obey God, Adam fell through disobedience and rebellion against God's instructions. Though Adam's transgression has affected all of humanity and natural existence, it has never abrogated the rule of God over His creation.

As mankind proliferated in the generations following Adam, mankind continued to drift further away from God and deeper into rebellion. In Noah's day, Noah alone submitted to the rule of God and obeyed His instructions to build an ark while warning others of impending judgment. After the Flood, God singled out a people to represent Him in the earth and point others to His rule and sovereignty. Abraham and his descendants were chosen to be that people to whom God would reveal Himself and establish a relationship. From the beginning they were told to obey, honor, and serve the God who had elevated them to a position of favor and blessing above the other nations of the earth.

> And now, Israel, what does the Lord your God require of you, but to fear the Lord your God, to walk in all His ways and to love Him, to serve the Lord your God with all your heart and with all your soul, and to keep the commandments of the Lord and His statutes which I command you today for your good? (Deut. 10:12-13).

As a nation in covenant relationship with God, Israel vacillated between obedience and rejection of God's commandments. Self-rule and self-determination were often embraced in place of submission to God's reign.

Many prophets were instructed by God to warn the people to return to Him and follow His ways. Again, and again, God revealed that He expected Israel, and indeed all of mankind, to pursue His will in their interaction with each other and their service to Him.

> He has shown you, O man, what is good; and what does the Lord require of you but to do justly, to love mercy, and to walk humbly with your God? (Mic. 6:8).

The Book of Ecclesiastes records Solomon's pursuit of meaning in life though the experience of every desire and pleasure. He carefully observed and noted the various nuances of human existence, often remarking that all was vanity. His concluding statements reveal that mankind's purpose for existence was not to be found in the self-centered experiences that mark many who live only for their own enjoyment and achievement. Rather, man's life is to be properly lived with God at the center.

> Let us hear the conclusion of the whole matter: Fear God, and keep his commandments: for this is the whole duty of man (Eccles. 12:13 KJV).

In the New Testament, Jesus reiterates the idea of man needing to live life in accordance with God's expectation. Matthew 22 records an attempt by the Pharisees to entrap Jesus in His teachings, hoping that He would say something politically incriminating against Caesar. When their scheme failed, they again questioned Him to identify the one great commandment in the Law of Moses.

> Jesus said to him, "You shall love the Lord your
> God with all your heart, with all your soul, and
> with all your mind. This is the first and great com-
> mandment. And the second is like it: You shall
> love your neighbor as yourself" (Matt. 22:37-39).

If God expects men in general to serve Him and to carry out His will, then it is even more expected of those who comprise His church. The redeemed are those who have responded to God's offer and provision of salvation from sin. They have acknowledged His sovereignty and surrendered their lives to the lordship of Christ. They have become participants in the proclamation of the gospel and the advancement of the kingdom of God on the earth. All that is done in ministry, as well as one's personal walk, is to be aimed at honoring and pleasing God. Though He calls, equips, and empowers men in the carrying out of His will, it must be remembered it is His will, not our own. In the local church, we are to serve and function for God's glory.

In Colossians chapter three, the apostle Paul points the believer to the type of character traits and behavior that should be seen in the redeemed. He acknowledg-es that prior to conversion they had exhibited ungodly behavior, but now they were to actively pursue righ-teous conduct. He repeatedly points them to God and Christ in the working out of their relationships with each other. They are told to forgive as Christ forgave, to give way to the rule of God's peace in their hearts, to be indwelt with the wisdom of Christ's Word, and to sing from their hearts to the Lord. The statement of verse 17 sums up the idea that all of their efforts are to be undertaken primarily for the glory of God.

> And whatever you do in word or deed, do all in
> the name of the Lord Jesus, giving thanks to God
> the Father through Him (Col. 3:17).

The physical action and verbal expression of committed Christians are to be directed toward honoring Christ. As they serve among their brethren in the local church, the members are to ensure that their motives are in line with his Lord's expectations. The name of Jesus must be cast in a good light by the behavior of the members of the church. The worth, dignity, and power of that name must be affirmed in worship, service, fellowship, and ministry. In doing so, members demonstrate appreciation to God for the gift of His Son.

A similar sentiment is expressed in Paul's directive to bondservants who were Christians in the Colossian churches. While not meant to approve of their status as slaves, the advice seeks to encourage them to glorify God even in their current position. They were to see their labor as unto the heavenly Master as opposed to earthly men. The instruction is applicable to believers and committed Christians who labor in the workplace and in the local church. Keeping God in view is a greater motivation to wholehearted service than seeking man's approval.

> And whatever you do, do it heartily, as to the
> Lord and not to men, knowing that from the Lord
> you will receive the reward of the inheritance; for
> you serve the Lord Christ (Col. 3:23-24).

Peter's first epistle also directs the believer to the idea of serving for God's glory. He opens the first chapter by recounting the hope that Christians possess because of God's mercy revealed through Christ Jesus.

The particular believers to whom he writes were facing trials and persecution in the first century, yet they could rejoice in God's providential care and protection. The hope of their salvation was a source of motivation to live obedient and holy lives before God. Submission to governing authorities, to earthly masters, to each other, and even suffering for righteousness could be better managed by the knowledge that Christ also submitted and suffered. In the fourth chapter, Peter reminds them that the end of all things is near and that they should demonstrate love and hospitality toward each other. Then he exhorts them regarding their service.

> As each one has received a gift, minister it to one another, as good stewards of the manifold grace of God. If anyone speaks, let him speak as the oracles of God. If anyone ministers, let him do it as with the ability which God supplies, that in all things God may be glorified through Jesus Christ, to whom belong the glory and the dominion forever and ever. Amen (1 Pet. 4:10-11).

Several things of note in Peter's instruction will aid committed Christians in serving in the proper manner and with the proper motive. First, those who possess a gift must recognize that it was given to them by God. It did not originate with them but was placed in them by the grace of God. As such, individuals must responsibly manage or be good stewards of the gift. They must know they are being held accountable by God for how they use what they have been given. Stewardship comes with accountability and demands responsibility.

Next, individuals must use their gifts in service to their fellow believers. They are to minister to those who will benefit from the exercise of the gift. The gift is not given for personal use, gratification, or exaltation, but for the support of others in the church. Teaching, singing, administrating, and helping are all intended for the benefit of the recipient. The church is built up, edified, and strengthened when committed Christians use their gifts to serve the kingdom of God. There is then a natural interconnectedness that is realized in the presence of gifts in the church. Gifted members need the church, so they have a place within which to exercise their gifts and demonstrate responsibility to the Lord. The church needs the members' gifts in order to benefit from the comfort, instruction, and inspiration that they bring.

Then, the exercise of the gifts by committed Christians must be empowered by the Lord. Peter says believers must speak as oracles of God. They must speak as the very utterance of God, which means they must allow God to speak through them. The preacher/teacher must be conscious of his or her status as a vessel that the Holy Spirit desires to use. Submission to and reliance upon the Holy Spirit in the preparation and the presentation will result in the utterance of God. Ministry must be done with a dependence upon divine ability. Human strength and resources are insufficient and vastly inferior to the demand of heavenly work. Though God uses human instruments, they stand in need of His divine empowerment to be effective. The power of the Holy Spirit is available in the exercise of our gifts so that we may accomplish spiritually what cannot be done naturally.

Finally, Peter's exhortation hints that in the successful exercise of our gifts, we should take no credit for ourselves but give all the glory to God. It is a powerful temptation for us to bask in the wonder of incredible accomplishment, as if we did it entirely on our own. The admiration and adulation that others may heap upon us can be intoxicating. But, we must always remember that we can do nothing without Christ's power through the Holy Spirit. He may have worked through us to benefit others, but the praise and honor ultimately belong to Him. The result of ministry and service in the church by those gifted is so God may be glorified through Christ Jesus.

Committed Christians must demonstrate a keen understanding of their responsibilities to serve in the church for the glory of God. The assigned duties and responsibilities may seem small and insignificant compared to others, but they are all necessary. God has positioned us where He wants us to be in Christ's body. He has also given us whatever gifts and abilities that we possess to be of service to the Kingdom. Committed Christians will be effective when they serve as unto the Lord, not as unto men. They will demonstrate good stewardship of their gifts by ministering to others with a dependence upon the Holy Spirit. They will take no credit for their successes but will direct and deflect all the glory to God.

## MEMBERSHIP ASSESSMENT

- Do you prefer to work in the spotlight or behind the scenes?
- Do you believe that God will judge you for your service as a believer?
- Are you fulfilled in your service to your church?
- Are you using all of your gifts in service to your church?

- How is God being glorified by your service to your local church?

## A FINAL CONSIDERATION

Author Craig Brian Larson relates an illustration that adequately reinforces the concept of serving for the glory of God:

*Dr. Paul Brand was speaking to a medical college in India on* Matthew 5:16: "Let your light so shine before men that they may see your good works and glorify your Father which is in heaven." *In front of the lectern was an oil lamp, with its cotton wick burning from the shallow dish of oil. As he preached, the lamp ran out of oil, the wick burned dry, and the smoke made him cough. He immediately used the opportunity.*

*"Some of us here are like this wick," he said. "We're trying to shine for the glory of God, but we stink. That's what happens when we use ourselves as the fuel of our witness rather than the Holy Spirit. Wicks can last indefinitely, burning brightly and without irritating smoke, if the fuel, the Holy Spirit, is in constant supply."*

# CONCLUSION

The importance of the local church cannot be under-stated. The Church universal is present and influential throughout the world through the collective efforts of local communities of faith. The members of the local church are the faces, the hands, the feet, and the voices that make up the body of Christ in a given community. Who Jesus is and what He represents will be revealed in the actions and attitudes of committed Christians.

If the return of Christ is to gather a perfected church, should we not make every effort to do our part in pursuing perfection? God's best and ultimate for us should be our aim. Individually, that means be-coming and achieving all that God has designed for us. At home, at work, in the community, and in the church, we should strive to be and do all that God has instructed in His Word. The world needs good people. It needs good husbands and wives, fathers and moth-ers, sons and daughters. It needs good employees and employers, laborers and managers, businessmen and craftsmen. The world needs good citizens living in and comprising its towns, cities, states, and countries. And the world needs good committed Christians submitted to God, reflecting Christ, and empowered by the Holy Spirit.

Good committed Christians hip could ideally result when mature believers carry out the mission of the King-dom through the local church. The reality is, however, that Christian maturity is an ongoing process that requires daily diligence and attention. The believer who walks with His Lord one day at a time and is provided stimulation to grow in the local church will make progress. In the same manner, good committed Christians hip will be cultivated by intentional teaching and training that points believers toward godly responsibility.

If the local church and believers are necessary to the overall mission of the kingdom of God, the FINISH Commitment, then committed Christians are vital to the local church's participation. Good local churches are made up of good local committed Christians. Good committed Christians are maturing believers who understand their responsibilities as citizens of God's kingdom. They are committed to the collective efforts of the local assembly and have been taught how to serve in their local church. May these principles and strategies form an invaluable guide to the productive service of your membership in your local church.

# Serve on Purpose: SPONSORS

Dr. J. David Stephens
COG Executive Committee Member
World Missions Liaison

| Administrative Bishops | State/Region |
| --- | --- |
| Dr. Mitchell Corder Jr. | Tennessee |
| Les Higgins | Ohio |
| Dr. Anthony Pelt | Cocoa, Florida |
| Thomas Madden | North Georgia |
| Thomas S. Gillum | South Carolina |
| David Munguía | Northwestern Hispanic |
| Dr. Kenneth Hill | Southern New England |
| Ronald Martin | Great Lakes |

A special thanks goes to all the individuals listed above from the International Executive Committee members and administrative bishops for their financial support toward the publication of the first Multicultural Education resource for the Global Church of God. Your contribution has helped us to provide the book in five languages; and without your help, this would not have been possible.

It is the intention of the Division of Education to provide for other books in more languages. Therefore, we would like to invite you to pray and/or partner with us to fulfill this goal.

You may send your contribution earmarked to:

Dr. Daniel J. Vassell Sr.
Multicultural Education Ministries
MCEM Book Language Publication
PO Box 2430
Cleveland TN 37320-2430
Email: mcem@cogdoe.org or Call. 423-478-7061

# PENTECOSTAL THEOLOGICAL SEMINARY
# ACADEMIC PROGRAMS

The Pentecostal Theological Seminary is a graduate school dedicated to preparing pastors, chaplains, and ministry leaders for global evangelization and Kingdom impact.

- ACCESSIBLE:   On-Campus • J-Terms • Sync • All Online • Cohorts
- AFFORDABLE:   Low Tuition • Financial Aid • Scholarships
- AVAILABLE:   Fulfill Your Ministry Goals

## MASTERS AND DOCTORAL PROGRAMS
- Master of Divinity (MDiv)
- Master of Arts in Clinical Mental Health Counseling (MACMHC)
- Master of Theological Studies (MTS)
- Master of Arts in Church Ministries (MACM)
- Master of Arts in Christian Studies (MACS)
- Master of Arts in Counseling (MAC)
- Doctor of Ministry (DMin)

- Certificate in Wesleyan-Pentecostal Ministry

## ACCREDITATION
- Association of Theological Schools (ATS)
- Southern Association of Colleges and Schools—Commission on Colleges (SACSCOC)
- Association for Hispanic Theological Education (AETH)
- Other Accrediting Agencies for Special Academic Programs

423.478.1131 • 800.228.9126   WWW.PTSEMINARY.EDU   INFO@PTSEMINARY.EDU

www.ingramcontent.com/pod-product-compliance
Lightning Source LLC
LaVergne TN
LVHW021354080426
835508LV00020B/2282